Divine Power Speaks
with the Buddha

Divine Power Speaks
with the Buddha

Dr. Thomas C. McGarrity

ISBN: 1507551274
ISBN 13: 9781507551271
Library of Congress Control Number:2015900791
CreateSpace Independent Publishing Platform
North Charleston, South Carolina

Table of Contents

Foreword

▲ ▲ ▲

Why the name Divine Power Speaks?

IN THE EARTHTRIBE TRADITION OF vision questing, there is a yearlong preparation, a year of integration, a year of helping others toward a quest for a new identity. As Dr. McGarrity well describes in this book, *Divine Power Speaks with the Buddha*, he embarked on such a journey wherein he, as a vision quester, hiked into a sacred, natural area in order to connect with that primal sub-personality that lies so close to the soul. What I sometimes call *the Wild Heart*. The intent of the quest was to link with and open to the sacred web of eco-fields, through which the Sacred Mystery sends information and meaning not only to Tom, the quester, but also for Mother Earth, Herself.

This wilderness quest offered a radically different perspective than many mystical traditional practices, in that it required Tom, the quester, to leave behind, if only for a day or more, the comforts of culture in order to submit to the challenges of the natural order. Sensual Nature became the primary conduit of enlightenment rather than an obstacle. Such a challenge was the purpose of the endeavor. In this vein, Tom brought with him his previous personality patterns (including other mystical experiences) and submitted himself to a small circle in a redwood forest with the aspiration that his identity would be expanded beyond his then current definition of himself. The first layer of such an experience is a profound sense of humility; in this pathway humans slowly realize that we are not dominants standing apart and abstract from Earth, but rather, humble participants, a vulnerable species among species.

When Tom was escorted back to the vision encampment to sit with a council of elders and process his time apart, he looked very different. A certain energetic radiance pulsated out of his being like bursts of sunlight through the limbs of the redwoods that were surrounding us. And no wonder! He had encountered with a top-of-the-food-chain creature and opened the way for a Sacred Voice from the depths and the heights to come through. The elders present were well aware that they were not "naming" Tom, but rather, listening closely to his narrative in which a new and larger identity was unfolding. In so doing, they meditated and agreed that there was, indeed, a clear Spirit Voice seeking to transmit through the experience. As with all vision questers, the elders cautioned Tom, now known to us as Divine Power Speaks, to walk with deep humility at having entered an altered state of consciousness and communicated with the Infinite. It might be easy in some instances to misread or inflate. Such is the role of community—to offer a context for the ongoing unfolding of the vision for the service of Mother Earth's well being. In this book, Dr. McGarrity takes us on a journey to an ever enlarging of consciousness and compassion, one in which, at certain moments, we may engage our own affinity with the Infinite.

Apapacho, Go well,

Will Taegel, Ph.D.
Dean
Wisdom School of Graduate Studies
Ubiquity University

Preface

▲ ▲ ▲

IN THE SPACE WHERE TEACHING, healing, counseling and coaching all intersect, there have been many explorers, pioneers, practitioners, followers, and even the Enlightened Buddha; and yet, humanity seems to remain in a never-ending state of infirmary. In a place of deeply profound prayerful meditation, in the place where the Voice of Divinity expresses so clearly to me, I was told to trumpet the practice of past-life regression. This little known healing modality, displaying remarkable healing results, can contribute to the end of human suffering. Furthermore, I was told that there are a number of sacred healing modalities that should be more fully exposed to suffering humanity. Following the guidance of the Voice, this book examines the findings of my sacred expeditions into the realms of dreams, vision quests, near-death experiences, altered states including labyrinth walking and holotropic breathwork, pilgrimages, and past and between-life regressions.

Once having crossed these powerful healing domains, and having become more familiar with our conversation with Divinity, we may come to see that surrendering to our Creator might actually be what is truly needed to end our suffering, or should we say, our sense of suffering. This book is our listening to this powerfully loving Voice. Enjoy!!

CHAPTER 1

Introduction

▲ ▲ ▲

OVERVIEW

This book is the result and expression of my direct access with the Divine, and this direct access to Divinity is what makes this work original. I gladly stand on the ground of the historic mystic tradition as my orientation. From before my very first days at the Wisdom School of Graduate Studies, I have been invited into remarkable and humbling conversations with our Creator. The clearest message was always that we should let go of our dependence on the intellect, and instead go to our deepest and most sacred place for wisdom and understanding of life and purpose. This consistent message truly defines what mysticism and the mystic are all about. You will see that I redefine the role of the intellect as supportive of the Divine Voice, rather than as the dominant factor in our mystical conversation.

This book is meant to be a road map for readers and spiritual researchers who are up for the challenge and willing to make the powerful choice of surrendering our beliefs and perceptions to the true Source from which we came. Having done so, we find ourselves in a mystical realm, living freely and harmoniously; one with all who inhabit this glorious planet, where suffering is not lasting or real.

This book is Divinely guided by design, method, and framework, and is assisted by experts in all the places that we shall visit. That is a startling claim, yet it will be clear how I support such a proposal as the book unfolds. Every effort will be made to allow you to feel participation in each of the many mystical experiences. The tone of the writing will first and foremost be subjective and interior and then move to a reflective perspective with other sources, with primarily attention paid to the Buddha, as seen through the work of Eknath Easwaran (1985). The ultimate goals are to better understand the true nature of our Divine relationship and to inspire transformational changes in the lives of readers and researchers alike.

I am aware that this approach is not usual for mainstream academia. Perhaps this is precisely why the Voice has led me to this groundbreaking work and is asking that it be done within the halls of the Wisdom School of Graduate Studies. I invite the University to journey with me into this novel domain as part of our reshaping academic inquiry.

My field of knowledge and orientation is mysticism. Mysticism is the belief that union with or absorption into the Deity or the Absolute, or the spiritual apprehension of knowledge inaccessible to the intellect, may be attained subjectively, through meditation, contemplation and self-surrender. My total and unconditional surrender to Divinity is what brought me into the mystical realms. My dual focus will be to invite you into each mystical experience with a reasoned reading that is intended to support rather than overwhelm the experience. This approach, then, takes our discovery into new territory where we are actually invited into a mystical state of consciousness rather than an intellectual consideration.

Placing Our Discovery In Context

A Mystic is a person who seeks by meditation, contemplation and self-surrender to obtain unity with or absorption into the Deity or the Absolute, and consequently believes in the spiritual apprehension of truths that are beyond the intellect. My direct access to the Divine came by invitation only. Once there, I knew that I could return with the questions that form the essence of our discovery process.

The Buddha sought to end human suffering twenty-five hundred years ago, and yet humanity seems to be suffering more than ever. All the greatest minds of science and medicine have sought and continue to seek for an end to human suffering. People primarily turn to drugs and alcohol or pills and weekly psychiatric sessions to end or at least dull the senses of their suffering. The time has come to enter the mystical realm and directly ask Divinity how to end our suffering. The time has come to enter the mystical realm to learn, once and for all, how to live peacefully and purposely on this glorious planet.

This book will take us on several powerfully mystical expeditions, and with deepest humility, we will directly ask our Creator how to end our suffering, as the Voice comes through a variety of channels including place, people and creatures. We will be assisted in our search from noted scientists who have blazed the trails that we will expand even further. Our surrender to the Divine allows our entry into the mystical realm for answers that were beyond the intellectual reach of these brave pioneers.

Conceptual Framework

Our work will take the form of sacred expeditions to under-appreciated but powerful modes of non-traditional healing that circumvent pills and weekly psychiatric sessions. We will visit dreams, altered states, near-death experiences, vision quests, pilgrimages, and past and between life regressions, and ask the Voice how to find healing in these places. We will call upon noted experts and pioneers in the fields of these healing modalities to assist us in our understanding of the context from which the Voice is speaking to us. And with the assistance of Easwaran's work in *The Dhammapada* (1985), we will carefully consider what the Buddha might say about each of these sacred expeditions, as a means of expanding the impact of these mystical revelations.

More On Easwaran's Dhammapada

Each chapter will end with words taken directly from The Dhammapada that might suggest what the Buddha may have thought of the particular concepts covered in the chapter. Eknath Easwaran, who transcribed The Dhammapada (1985), is a pre-eminent student of the mystics. Coming to the United States from India as a Fulbright Scholar in 1959, for nearly 40 years he taught, authored, translated and drew deep inspiration from the sacred literature of mystics of all spiritual traditions. He developed, taught and practiced a method called passage meditation, which involves focusing the mind on inspiring sacred texts coming from the much-loved saints, sages, and scriptures of the Christian, Hindu, Sufi, Jewish, Native American, Buddhist, and Taoist traditions. Having authored over two-dozen books, his works are being read through more than twenty languages all around the world. Easwaran is a valuable window into mysticism and the mystics of all traditions.

We will use the work of Eknath Easwaran as the means through which we will view one of the most acclaimed mystics of all time, the Buddha. We will not be studying Buddhism, as much of its coverage represents mostly interpretations, philosophies, dogmas and doctrines of what people thought the Buddha had said. We are only interested in what the Buddha actually said to us in The Dhammapada. Easwaran believes that of all that was written about the beliefs and teachings of the Buddha, The Dhammapada is the truest and purest record of what the Buddha offered to humanity. Additionally, Easwaran's (1985) translation of The Dhammapada is considered by many to be one of the most authoritative renderings of this powerful material.

We will notice that in spite of the powerful messages that were brought to us by the Buddha, humanity continues its state of endless suffering. Why? We will explore a fresh approach that includes and transcends the Buddha's essential message. We will probe new experiences brought to us by the Divine Voice that may actually end suffering. The Buddha surrendered to the mind through meditation to find his freedom from suffering. We are being told by the Voice of Divinity that by fully surrendering to our Creator, we may find that we are not truly suffering after all. Let's listen to what the Voice has to say to us. Let's take our time and let these deep thoughts soak in.

CHAPTER 2

Sojourns into Dreamland

▲ ▲ ▲

MY SOJOURNS INTO DREAMLAND CAME through two sacred journeys first in Oakland, California and then in Maui, Hawaii, focusing on the wisdom, love and healing that come directly through the sharing of dreams within a group dynamic. These sojourns were preceded by acquainting myself with the dream terrain through writings by noted experts in the world of dreams, including the teachers on site as well as others in the field. It quickly became quite clear that the dreams are important and are the content of the group work, but that the group sharing is the context from which the meaningful messages appear. In other words, the Voice speaks as the group is in the process of sharing what came through individual dreams.

PRESENTERS ON DREAMWORK

Assisting the Voice in Oakland on the first sojourn were Dr. Jeremy Taylor, a Unitarian minister and author, who has worked tirelessly in the forefront of dream healing for almost forty years, and Dr. Bruce Silverman, a renowned drummer, teacher and artist-ritual healer. On the second sojourn in Maui came the assistance of Dr. Will Taegel, author, shaman, former Chair of the Texas State Board of Examiners in Psychotherapy and Dean of the Wisdom School of Graduate Studies, Dr. Apela Colorado, founder of the Worldwide Indigenous Science Network and a long time leader of Western-Indigenous educational efforts, and Dr. Daniel Deslaurier, a professor, noted researcher and co-founder of the Montreal Center for the Study of Dreams. At all times, the space was incredibly sacred, in part by the devotion of these fine teachers or guides and in part by the devout intentions of those in attendance.

SOJOURN IN OAKLAND

In my first sojourn into dreamland, Jeremy Taylor laid out very specific intellectual foundations along with archetypes for us to hold in mind as we approached the enactment of group dreamwork. High on his list were the following:

- All dreams speak a universal language and come in the service of health and wholeness.
- Only the dreamer can say with certainty what meanings his or her dream may have.
- There is no such thing as a dream with only one meaning.
- No dreams come just to tell you what you consciously already know.
- All dream group participants should agree at the outset to maintain anonymity in all discussions of dreamwork.
- And perhaps the most practical of all, when talking to others about their dreams, it is both wise and polite to preface your remarks with the words to the effect, "If it were my dream...," and to keep this commentary in the first person as much as possible. (lecture, Aug. 2011)

These terrain-setting perspectives became of great importance as my wife and I later incorporated them into our weekly spiritual study group dynamic.

Bruce Silverman spoke of and demonstrated the value of utilizing ritual, sound, and sacred drama into dreamwork. Ideally, the dream groups incorporate elements of gestalt work, sacred drama, mythology and play into dream re-enactment facilitation. The dream archetypes are very energetically welcomed, sung, danced and ultimately, lived, through his group process (lecture, Aug. 2011). The energy of the room was always very apparent when we practiced Bruce's method of dreamwork. We seemed to bring to life a most surreal dreamlike energy as our re-enactments came alive.

I use the word stimulating to describe both processes, because, whether the group was verbally re-enacting or physically re-enacting the dream, the participants were clearly stimulated. Of course, we were hoping to bring the dreamer to some resolution and meaning. But somehow, in both Jeremy Taylor's and Bruce Silverman's methods, we were drawn into the energy of the dream, the energy of the healing, and I would say, the energy of the Voice, Itself. It was very clear to me that each time that we worked through a dream, the dreamer felt a true sense of healing. These were not gentle taps on the shoulder. Rather, the dreamer was dramatically moved to tears and came to rather clear-cut moments of clarity. Perhaps more surprisingly, there seemed to be another group member who was visibly moved at the same time. This second person seemed to have need for a healing of his or her own. An unexpected third healing seemed to come to all those participating in the healing effort. We were allowed to heal in our own individual ways. It was as though the acts of kindness that we were showing to the dreamer were circling back to us in powerful and unexpected ways.

Jeremy Taylor might argue that the very nature of "If it were my dream..." thinking brings about a true living of the dream in our individual and real perspectives. So, it is not at all surprising that each member of the dream group would find himself or herself healed through each person's own moment, whether it came on the spot or at some later point in time. In any case, what I want to make clear is that I witnessed and experienced healings across the board, some visible and some indirect, but all very powerful.

Taylor mentioned that the conscious practice of prayer, meditation and contemplation, yoga and the like, focused on important life choices, will lead to richer, more vividly remembered and understood dream life. This seems like more than just practical advice. The stronger message seems to be that spending time in sacred places or incorporating sacredness into one's life might matter when it comes to understanding and appreciating the Voice's messages that are coming through the dreams.

It is also helpful to keep a dream journal and to write down the narrative of what went on in the experience, right then, in the night, as soon as possible in order to capture enough information on the spot. The dreamer can then review his or her scribbles in the morning, and more details can flow onto the notes, jogging even more memory of the dream. More details seem to come through the next few days.

Carl Jung says through Taylor, "The only way to verify any explorer's reports is to travel the territory and see for ourselves" (lecture, Aug. 2011). The dreamer is the only one who can really say for sure what or why they experienced what they experienced. The dream group can assist the process and does feel for themselves what the dream means to them, but the dreamer, the individual is the only one, for certain, who knows what is real. I think that Jeremy Taylor makes a crucial point when he commented on not needing to consult a "guru" for answers because, "It was your dream in the first place, and only you know what the dream means" (lecture, Aug. 2011). But, the Voice did bring the dream group together and speaks through its compassionate intentions to help the dreamer find resolution.

Staying with this train of thought, one might ask, "Why does this particular dream come up at this particular moment in time?" Well, magically, it always seems to happen just that way. In describing a particular person's dream, Taylor said, "It had yielded this amazingly elegant and succinct metaphor of what the dreamer perceived to be his greatest problem at that moment" (lecture, Aug. 2011).

Staying a bit longer on this point, one might ask, "How does one actually know what the dream means?" Jeremy Taylor spoke of the *Aha* moment: "In that moment, you remember consciously for the first time, what you already knew unconsciously that the dream meant at the time it first occurred" (lecture, Aug. 2011). Further, "the *Aha* is often accompanied by noticeable and immediate increased physical healing or need for healing" (lecture, Aug. 2011). The dream makes a very clear statement through the *Aha* sensation, that you are onto something very important. Even in nightmares, the dream is alerting the dreamer to pay attention, this is important! As Jung says through Jeremy Taylor, "The thing that cures a neurosis must be as convincing as the neurosis" (lecture, Aug. 2011). But sometimes, in order to fully heal, we must push on through and see what we really need to see.

When Taylor spoke on the courage to continue, he said, "To reach this level of healthy, whole experience and understanding, every step of the way must be traversed and whenever we succeed in removing a roadblock, the dreams skip ahead to the next place that needs repair work" (lecture, Aug. 2011). Having seen the dream, we can re-orient ourselves to take advantage of what we learned, reframing our waking lives and activities in line with what our dreams are telling us.

DEVELOPING A DREAM CIRCLE

My wife and I host a weekly spiritual study group. I was so moved by the healing that I witnessed through my participation in the first dreamland sojourn, that we decided to make dream sharing the next year's study topic. We worked through one dream each week, and I cannot tell you how beautiful the group experiences have been. I cannot say that I am surprised, but I am very, very pleased with what we witnessed from the group. I recently asked a group member to recall a dream that we discussed during our year of dreamwork. Even with several years since the dream, she shared her stunning recollection:

I am on a really tall building like a skyscraper and am leaning against the guardrail. Suddenly it gives way and I am falling backwards. I am really scared at first, but then realize that something or someone is cradling me and I am floating or flying in the air. I am safe and feel the most amazing joy and peacefulness that I have ever experienced. It is as if I am surrounded in a cloud of love and feel physical and mental bliss. I am floating over the big city down below, I open my eyes to take a look, but I am more content to just close my eyes and enjoy the moment. (Member of dream group, Oct. 2011)

The next week she added this follow-up dream:

I am in a room with you, and we are talking. You tell me that I can fly, but I say no way, it is not possible. You encourage me to give it a try, so I leap into the air and I am able to float or fly around the room. I feel powerful and energized, like I can do anything! (Member of dream group, Oct. 2011)

It seems to me that the Voice is stamping the first dream with this second dream. It seems to be saying, "Believe in your dream, believe in yourself."

Following the dream discussions, we did group meditation. The best way that I can describe the impact on the dreamer is to say that after the meditation, when the other group members were coming back to full awareness, the dreamer's eyes were big, bright and sparkling like diamonds, radiating love. She had a huge grin on her face. Similar reactions came from each of the dreamers in their particular weeks. All the members of the group seemed to feel a joy inside for having helped to bring such visible healing to the dreamers.

DREAM HEALING

Before we move to the second sojourn into dreamland, I must share a very real and powerful dream story that is living and breathing as I write these words. Last fall I had a very epic, Joseph Campbell hero's journey-style dream. I do not normally dream in this fashion, so, what I am about to share truly stood out in my awareness. In the dream, I was asked to hold up the earth's atmospheric dome so that the inhabitants would not perish from lack of oxygen. During the night I felt the lack of oxygen that was being foreshadowed. The next day, a dear friend entered the hospital and twelve days later passed away with oxygen deficiency as the ultimate cause. Naturally, I connected her passing with my dream and left it at that.

But the winter came and every cold or flu that I encountered seemed to result in a respiratory problem for me. At one time, my doctor showed concern about the low oxygen level in my bloodstream. Seeing his concern, I told him my dream. You can imagine his reaction. Here we were in the middle of cold or flu season, he had probably seen dozens of patients exhibiting symptoms similar to mine, and I suggested to him that we take my dream seriously and run additional tests.

Thankfully, my doctor played along with me and scheduled three additional tests. The blood test showed that my body chemistry was in very good shape. I had no cholesterol, diabetes, organ or glandular issues, whatsoever. Furthermore, I do not drink, smoke and do exercise daily. The breathing test showed that a hit on the inhaler helped my breathing, which was a likely outcome for most people.

The third test, an echo-cardiac stress test, was delayed a few months for a variety of reasons. But during those months, I noticed increasing difficulty in my breathing. One additional dream came along that included my deceased dad and had death as its main topic. This dream stirred me to use the telephone the next morning and schedule my stress test.

A few days later, I found myself on a treadmill in the cardiac unit of my local hospital. Feeling no pain but noticing the concern on the face of the cardiologist as he viewed the EKG results, I next found myself being whisked to the operating room for immediate cardiac surgery. It turns out that my right coronary artery was completely clogged, deformed and required three stents to properly secure it. I am presently in cardiac rehabilitation three days a week and working on balancing my body in terms of medications and exercise. Naturally, my family and I are delighted for me to be here to tell this tale. So that is it, a happy ending to this dream story? Not yet. There is more.

A friend of mine was quite taken by this story of an epic dream, leading to a stress test, leading to cardiac surgery, leading to healing, recovery and wholeness, He told a friend of his, and they agreed to take a simple but effective cardiac test. My friend's results showed that his blood pressure was too high, and his doctor upped his medications. Happy ending? There is more. His friend's results showed a ninety-seven percent clogged "widow-maker" left coronary artery that was too deformed for stents and required nearly immediate bypass surgery. Coincidentally, my wife and I were visiting my friend and his wife the day after his friend learned of his condition and plans for surgery. Again coincidentally, we ended up dining at the same restaurant the next night and were able to meet his friend and family two nights before his bypass surgery. The feeling while shaking his hand and looking into the eyes of his family members went beyond words.

If we look back on this epic dream story, we see the work of the Divine Voice alerting me of the need to pursue my breathing to the place where the clogged coronary artery was clearly noticeable to the cardiologist. Then, the sharing of the dream with the friend called the Voice into action again as my friend felt compelled to advise his friend to another successful cardiac outcome. While the content of these two segments of this story are clearly medical, I contend that there is a bigger message coming to us from the Voice. It seems to me that we are being told to learn to listen to the Voice, that there is a Divine conversation going on perpetually, and if we can acquire the ability to tune into the Divine frequency, that we will find ourselves protected, supported and guided throughout our human experience.

Sojourn In Maui

My second sojourn into the sacredness of dreamland took place in Maui, Hawaii and revealed layers upon layers of meaning in the dreams that we shared in group. But before describing these layers of revelation, let me take a moment to speak on the sacredness of the place that I was at during this second sojourn. There is no doubt in my mind that I was deeply planted in the sacred when, out of the blue, I was asked to rinse the feet of the participants as they crossed from a sacred practice event on the beach and returned to the gathering room. We wanted to be sure to honor the grounds of the Buddhist mission where our discussions were being held. Not tracking sand throughout their facilities was one way of showing our respect. With a simple garden hose in one hand and the foot of each group member in the other, I found myself more than just removing the sand. Somehow, the actual touch of the feet and toes with my fingers and the cleaning and all was quite a bit more than rinsing off the sand. I could tell that some people really enjoyed the experience. It was something like a spa treatment, I guess. To others, it seemed that they had to let go of their inhibitions and let a man touch and hold their foot. To others it was a ticklish moment that they either enjoyed or tolerated. It was definitely much more than rinsing sand off feet. Not to be overly melodramatic, what flashed in my mind was the reference to Jesus washing the feet of His apostles. The powerful feeling was about the love that I felt while honoring my brothers and sisters. So, while my back was not so pleased to have been bent over for such a stretch of time, my heart was overcome with love for each member of our group, as I simply rinsed their feet.

Another sacred and moving moment came when visiting the ancient petroglyphs. Apela Colorado, being intimately aware of the indigenous history of this island, shared with us how these ancient sketches, carved into these ancient rock formations, had been left as messages for future spiritual souls along this Hawaiian path in ways perhaps similar to Egyptian hieroglyphics (lecture, Jan. 2012). But as importantly to me, she spoke of how careless people had badly neglected and disrespected these sacred messages from indigenous minds of old. It was the neglect and disrespect that really touched me deeply. Alone on one of the rocks, I gave a hug and apologized for my ignorant human brothers, who had acted so thoughtlessly. From that hug came a true feeling of connection. I then saw more than just the carvings in the rocks. I saw images and faces of humans and animals alike. The final vision was of water that I took as tears on the rock. I gently wiped away the tears, expressed my heart-felt compassion and said my good-byes.

CIRCLE OF GRACE IN MAUI.

Another moving moment came while participating in a Circle of Grace ceremony during our stay in Maui. A group of us made a drive to a spiritually special place, which seemed to me like a burial ground overlooking a valley and the sea. It was visually impressive and spiritually moving at the same time. I found myself sitting on the ground in a meditative way. Suddenly, I felt myself rocking back and forth very noticeably and with a very perceivable rhythm. It was as though I was riding a horse across a wide expanse. This was not a visual experience, but rather, a powerfully physical one. I seemed to be riding my horse with great speed and enthusiasm. It was such a déjà vu-like moment that I had to open my eyes to see if I was actually on a horse. Of course, I was not, but the feelings were surreal.

Time passed and the group descended the hill to where our cars were parked. However, before we arrived at the parking lot, we came across a fenced area that I had not noticed on the way up the hill. Standing at the closest spot to our path were two beautiful brown horses. Most of the group had already passed this spot by the time that I came upon it. I touched and spoke with the horses and felt very comfortable with them.

CONNECTIONS TO THE WEB

Suddenly, another powerful déjà vu-like thought swept over me that seemed to involve these same horses. In the memory, I was staying at a little motel in a very small town in southwest Washington State. I was there for the funeral of a dear friend's wife (actually, she was a dear friend as well). The original purpose of the trip had been to say good-bye to the woman, who was overcome with liver cancer. I arrived on Friday morning to find that she had passed on Thursday night. So, the purpose of the trip shifted to comforting, consoling and support-ing my friend. Naturally, he was busy with arrangements and his own grief, so we spent just a little time together each day. The funeral was planned for Monday, and I was happy to stay an extra day. The funeral was then changed to Wednesday, and we discussed whether or not I would stay or head home. I left it totally up to my friend, who had some trouble deciding. Finally, I said that I would stay for the service and fly home on Thursday.

For almost a week, I spent an hour or so a day with my friend and the rest of the time wondering why I was there. The funeral came along, and I found myself sitting in the middle of a group of people whom I had never met. The minister asked for people to offer remembrances of the deceased woman. Except for her husband and son, nobody spoke. To me this felt extremely awkward. The minister was about to proceed with the service when I bolted out of my seat and spoke.

I introduced myself and said that I had already mourned the loss of my friend's wife months ago when they moved from Sedona to Washington State. Coming from Chicago, we had only spent three or four long-winded dinners together when my wife and I would come to Sedona for retreat; and yet, something in me missed them as if they had passed away. So, standing in the church, I shared that I did not feel sad, but I did feel love. I felt the love that they had for her, the love that she had for them and the Love that God had for all of us. Well, that opened the floodgates and many people then stood and shared. It was a beautiful remembrance of her life and times. The "why I was there" became instantly clear to me.

Back to the horses ... Each morning, two beautiful brown horses wandered over to my motel room window just to stand for a while. They belonged to a farmer, whose barn was a hundred or so yards away. They came by just to keep me company, I think. I opened the motel room window so that we could be more closely connected. The very same loving feelings were with me in Washington and Maui with these two beautiful brown horses. Do we think that they are the same ones?

Why did I tell this last story? What did it have to do with Dreamland? Inside this very sacred space the lines between waking life and dream life are sometimes blurred. Daniel Deslaurier gave two quotes in class that are significant at this point: As Henry David Thoreau said, "I do not know how to distinguish between our waking life and our dream life" (lecture, Jan. 2012). Also, from Fyodor Dostoyevsky came, "What does it matter whether it was a dream or reality, if the dream made known to me the truth" (lecture, Jan. 2012)?

Perspectives On Dreams

The perspective on dreams that I brought to this second sojourn was basically that dreams have a spiritual purpose. I believe that dreams are a form of expression of the Voice that is helping, guiding and supporting the progress of our soulful beings. I believe that the Voice is communicating to us in a mentoring, advising, coaching way.

Deslaurier made a rather keen observation that half the world sleeps or dreams while the other half lives the waking life (lecture, Jan. 2012). Of course, we switch places as night falls for some and sun rises for others. He suggested that there was a natural connectivity of humans who live in a world where sleeping or dreaming and waking alternate in such a way, as if, we are all working together and taking turns playing the simplest roles that we play–dreamer and liver. He spoke of how dreams inform our waking lives, and conversely, how our waking lives inform our dreams. Deslaurier suggested that there was a natural give and take and its resulting growth or evolution coming through this alternating of valuable insights that we give and receive (lecture, Jan. 2012).

Will Taegel shared great insights into the many ways in which the *Mother Tongue* is speaking to us (Taegel, 2012). Dreams were certainly part of this Voice, but so were so many more ways in which we can listen and learn, ultimately, leading to happier and more purposeful lives on this beautiful planet. Reading of signs and omens, visions and dreams, nature-based community, nature-based ceremony, songs and chants of the ancients, rhythms and body movements, our newest evolution of scientists speaking to us in a new language, human and natural architecture, all of which taken individually and with careful attention can alter significantly our understanding of what we are all about and why we are here.

Apela Colorado spoke of the great value of participating in group-dream sharing. She spoke of how the individual dreams that we all seem to have can be visibly connected to one another's dreams, and the composite dream that comes forth is one of great value to the group and beyond (lecture, Jan. 2012). The Voice seems very much alive in this sense and invites us to join in a much more collective, rather than individual, way of living on this planet.

EXERCISES ON DREAMING

At one point on this sojourn, the large group of us was asked to head into a sacred and meditative place within, to pull up an image from a recent dream. We then spent time getting comfortable with the dream before bringing it to the group. Each dream initially came to the large group through small groups of three. Taking turns within the threesomes, we shared our dreams.

Each threesome had a dream teller, a questioner, and an observer, whom we called, "elder." The point of the questioner was to pull every last drop of significance from the dream teller by simply asking, "Is there more?" At the end of each dream sharing, the elder shared what he or she thought the dream meant. The dream teller ultimately decided what it meant, but the interaction of the two viewpoints was rather amazing. Roles were rotated, and all three dreams were shared and discussed.

Whole dreams were not brought back to the big group, but rather, simple truths were brought back. Interesting group discussion was had before a composite dream was literally woven together from the singular truths that came back from the threesomes. I would say that the end result was each person came away with a much, much bigger perspective than they would have from merely thinking through their individual dream by himself or herself.

There were so many valuable characteristics to this dream exercise, all of which centered on the connecting with others in creating a significant meaning from what seemed to be very individual dreams. The sacred meditation brought an important dream to each person. The threesomes brought the

fullness out of each dream, and the most significant piece of the most significant dream to the larger group. So, this exercise started with a number of very
individual dreams and ended with a beautiful dream tapestry representing the
finest of what the group had brought forth to be shared with one another and
beyond.

RECOLLECTIONS

Looking back, there seemed to be more than just dreams being woven together
into a dreaming tapestry It is as though the Voice was weaving the participants
together into a most amazing, living, breathing tapestry. What were once many
individual thoughts and isolated interests became one large and beautiful man-
dala of dreams. Tibetan monks would be proud.

Another splendid group effort had its focus on the many significant layers
that dreams contain and the value of the group's sorting through each and every
layer for meaning. This exercise began with a sacred and meditative moment,
which created individual images that were expanded into a dream-like story.
The large group split into dyads to work through the individual images. The
listener continuously asked, "Who are you?" This took the image or dream as
deep as possible. The large group then gathered back together for purposes of
working through a single volunteer's dream. The new focus was on how many
layers of a dream we could work through. We touched on every detail of every
scene. We thoroughly discussed every symbol, every feeling, and every reaction
to every thought that came up. When we were all finished with the dream, we
thoroughly discussed what this particular dream and all of its layers meant to us
individually, and then, more importantly, to us collectively. The Voice clearly
speaks through the collective.

These recollections on the exercises draw me back to one of the books that
I read prior to this sojourn, *Healing Dreams* (2000) by Marc Ian Barasch, because

to me, the greatest gifts of dreams are the healing and transformations that they help to facilitate. This book was delightfully filled with stories of healing and transformational dream. While most of Barasch's stories were about individuals learning from these powerfully visual dreams, he also shared stories that point out the collective nature of dreams and dream societies. A favorite quote from Barasch goes, "Perhaps, in the end, there are no dreams intrinsically more healing than those that demonstrate that our separation is an illusion; that we are part of a living web that extends beyond our own skin and skull" (2000, p. 122). Barasch spoke of how indigenous and native cultures valued and used dreams in everyday life. He spoke of cultures of past and present eras that listened intently to villagers' dreams as significant signals for making important tribal decisions. The cultures that Barasch mentioned spanned the whole globe, including North, South and Latin American tribes, people from all parts of Asia, Africa and the Islands. He spoke of the Invisible Community and of modern day "helping professionals" working with indigenous societies, shamans and other healers. Lastly, Barasch (2000) spoke of how healing dreams may circulate, issuing from the dream world to the individual, from the individual to society, and from society back to the individual, gathering momentum as it goes. That brings a powerful spiraling energy to mind that cannot help but have healing effects.

GIFTS OF GRACE

These sacred sojourns through dreams have moved me deeply. To my way of thinking, the Voice spoke to me and provided meaningful messages to be shared with my brothers and sisters. It was always clear to me that I was in sacred space. It was clear to me that I entered of my own volition; but also, that my presence was anticipated and welcomed. It was as though the choice was always mine to enter or not enter. But the Voice seemed to always be ready for my arrival. In a subtle way, there was a great feeling of support in that silent interchange between the Voice and me.

On each and every day of these sojourns, something mystical seemed to present itself for my appreciation and acceptance. When I boil down the essence of these messages, I come back to the notion that dreams are very important. They are a gift to us. They serve a valuable purpose. They come through a different language than we are normally used to hearing. They need to be paid attention. We need to share with like-minded people to benefit individually and collectively. What seems important is that we value them for their guidance and direction and for their inspiration and support as we try to navigate through challenging lifetimes.

The biggest question is a rhetorical one, "Where do the messages of these dreams come from?" I say this should be rhetorical because deep reflection is called for on such a weighty topic. At the same time, having been through these sacred sojourns, I feel that I do come back with an answer.

The clearly noticeable benefits of these dreams are wisdom and understanding, loving feelings, and healing or support through challenging times. These benefits seem to come as personal gifts to us. They are gifts of grace that are delivered mystically to us. They have the power to change the very course of our lives, particularly at times when change is desperately needed. So, who would be the mystical giver of such precious gifts to us? Who cares enough about us to pay attention to when we might need such wisdom, love and healing support? Who knows us better than we even know ourselves, and who cares enough to offer unconditional love and support to us along the way?

I think that we all know the answer to these questions. I think that we all know who knows us and loves us beyond our own capacities for love and support. I think that it is up to us to follow the Voice of this Divine giver of gifts and share unconditional love and support to all those around us.

REFLECTIONS ON THE BUDDHA

The Buddha does not mention dreams, per se, in The Dhammapada. He does not mention any of the expeditions that we will review, for that matter. But one particular verse from The Dhammapda stands out in my mind when I think about our sojourns into dreamland. From the verse called, The Wise, comes, "If you see someone wise, who can steer you away from the wrong path, follow that person as you would one who can reveal hidden treasures. Only good can come out of it" (Easwaran, 1985, p. 126). The following of this "some-one" comes incredibly close to what I consider the following of the Voice in our dreamwork conversation.

In my own personal dream about holding up the atmosphere dome against planetary oxygen deficiency, which led to my breathing issues, that led to successful cardiac surgery and healing, I certainly felt steered away from dismissing the medical condition and to-wards the eventual surgical solution. I sense that the Buddha would have supported my efforts of listening to this "someone" and as a result, living to continue helping others along the way.

In the dreams that my study group friend experienced, I sensed that the Buddha would have supported the notion that she was not only free to fly, but that she should believe in herself as the Voice advised her to do. While the Buddha's method called for deep medi-tation, which often is seen as an independent action, I can not help but think that the collective nature of the group dream dynamic would have appealed to the Buddha, for He certainly found Himself in the company of a large group of monks.

CHAPTER 3
Trips into Altered States of Consciousness

▲ ▲ ▲

MY TRIPS INTO ALTERED STATES of consciousness were several and powerful. The writings of noted experts in their fields provided helpful context from which the Voice could be better understood. The trips themselves were varied in intensity and message, but all clearly came through sacred space, and were meant to be shared in this writing.

HOLOTROPIC BREATHWORK

Holotropic Breathwork, the final destination of this sacred trip, was developed by Stanislav Grof, M.D., who studied medicine and psychoanalysis at the Charles University School of Medicine in Prague in the early 1950s. In the 1960s, Dr. Grof became a principle investigator in a clinical study of the possible therapeutic potential of a psychedelic drug provided by Sandoz Pharmaceuticals.

Dr. Grof came into his own just as this large Swiss pharmaceuticals company was interested in testing their LSD drug as part of the research program on which Grof was working. Very quickly, Stan saw and understood the incredible opportunity to offer so-called incurable patients therapy in ways that they had never experienced before. Years and years of fruitless conversation could be overstepped by one fantastic view of consciousness. Perhaps equally importantt, doctors, nurses and therapists could have a glimpse of what the patient was actually going through, that they previously had only read or heard about, but had never actually experienced for themselves. A chemical-based, spiritual form of therapy had opened up to unbelievable opportunities for much needed healing. Unfortunately, the communists of Eastern Europe, where this breakthrough work was taking place, had no tolerance for the spiritual side effects being offered by these psychedelics. So, off Stan went to the United States.

In 1967, Dr. Grof became an Assistant Professor at Johns Hopkins University and the Chief of Psychiatric Research at the Maryland Psychiatric Research Center in Baltimore, Maryland, where he hooked up with Abraham Maslow, the father of humanistic psychology in America. Maslow had introduced the healing benefits of self-realization and self-actualization in the 1950s and was breaking ground in the realm of spontaneous mystical experiences in the 1970s. Enters Stan Grof and transpersonal psychology is born.

A new acceptance of spirituality and metaphysics was emerging, with a larger view of reality, and was very different from materialistic science, yet perfectly correlated with Aldous Huxley's perennial vision and the emerging field of quantum science that was coming to life. Therapeutic healing, personal transformation and consciousness evolution were circling round each other in this new scientific paradigm, which, of course, challenged the old guard, western industrial mainstream scientific community to no end. Rather than welcoming the healing benefits of these non-ordinary states of consciousness, they labeled them pathologies and even outlawed some of them. However, Stan Grof was already bitten by the holotropic (moving towards wholeness) "bug" and quickly saw its characteristics similar to what shamans of the native cultures described in their non-linear rites of passage ceremonies and practices. In fact, the various triggers to the holotropic states, drumming, fasting, sleep and space deprivation, vision questing and psychedelic plants were not new at all to the shamanic-led communities, for they may have been with man since the dawn of time. Grof's groundbreaking therapy, called holotropic breathwork (which I will describe shortly in greater detail through my personal trip), allowed him to circumvent outlawed LSD research, and instead, follow the path of the shamanic healers of new and old, into a therapy that included shamanic music, drumming and deep breathing that evoke spiritual visions, drawings and long lasting healing.

By taking on the mainstream science community, particularly in the areas of psychology and psychotherapy, Dr. Grof was taking on the deep seeded beliefs of Freud and his followers. It was not so much that Grof did not appreciate their work, but from his holotropic sessions were coming much deeper levels of healing inquiry and results. The model of adult issues coming from adolescent traumas, coming from post-natal, child and mother issues, was fine, but much more was coming out of his patients. The holotropic breathwork was allowing his patients to revisit traumas that occurred prior to the moment of birth, in the womb, during cervix-closed contractions, struggling through the birth canal, and the cutting of the umbilical cord, which are incredibly difficult moments for the psyche that the Freudian model never truly accepted. So, it was not that Stan was replacing the Freudian work, so much, as he was adding to it by including what his patients were sharing in these most dramatic therapeutic sessions. In other words, the roots of the patients' problems grew much deeper than their early mother and child interactions. Curiously to me, and according to Grof, the deepest roots often showed to be not of this lifetime, but of past lives, a notion that I have witnessed time and time again through past life regression work.

An example that Stan Grof gave went as follows: A chronic asthmatic sufferer, through holotropic breathwork (HB) might reveal a near drowning at age seven, then a whooping cough at age two, choking in the birth canal, and finally, a strangulation or hanging in a past life. Each of these revelations came from deeper and deeper moments in the HB session or therapy. The recognition of the deep root cause, as witnessed in the past life vision, would be all that was necessary for the patient to be cured of this seemingly never ending battle with breathing. This sort of result came about time after time. It is no wonder that Grof placed so much faith in his new therapeutic method.

Example Of Healing And Its Roots

In a very similar vein, I had a twenty-three year old friend who was deathly afraid of the water. Swimming, boating, the beach or any water-related activities were out of the question, as panic would set in. That was the case until taking her into a past life and seeing that she had met her death as the result of drowning. We talked about the fact that the fear of water was legitimate as she *had* drowned, but the drowning had occurred in that past life and need not continue to terrorize her in this current life. To test the theory, she reluctantly agreed to go with me to my swim club for a couple of swim lessons. She apprehensively walked down the steps into the pool, but within two short lessons, she was swimming like a fish. The fear was completely replaced by exuberance and confidence. The friend was so proud of herself that she hurried to call her mother with her great news.

In Stan Grof's example and my story, the keys to the healings were the recognition of what was truly causing the problems. Once seen by the patients, the healings happened on their own, or with a little bit of coaching by the therapist or me. This concept was not lost on Grof. He saw that holotropic technique helped to allow a form of spiritual inner radar (as he calls it) which brings forth areas of the psyche that need current attention and helps connect them to their root causes for the ultimate healings. Revisiting a past life scene is easy enough, as the patient merely ends up in the memory bank of a particular past life that seems to come forth through the spiritual inner radar or Voice, in my experience. Group dreamwork, which we have already visited, is another relatively easy way to allow the spiritual inner radar or Voice to bring forth a particular dream, which the group can assist in ferreting out meaning.

In medicine, diagnosis leads to standard treatment to cure standard disease. In psychiatry, symptoms and syndromes are studies, not diseases. And the variety of possibilities seems endless, which is why patients tend to remain in weekly therapy for so very long. The never-ending forty-five minute conversation with therapist has very little chance of resolving patient problems any time soon. But Stan Grof and other holotropic healers produced remarkable results in very quick fashion, because the healing was happening of its own, as a result of calling upon the spiritual inner radar, what I commonly refer to as the Voice, who is helping you along the pathway home. Fears, depressions, anxieties, etc. were seen as blockages that simply needed some way of releasing in order for the patient to resume his or her life and continue on the path. Holistic healers have known this to be true of the physical body and have used acupuncture and other forms of energy healing for many, many centuries. The same applications were working with mental and emotional healings thanks to Grof and many others of his ilk.

A New Philosophy

With this new healing modality came a new healing philosophy, that the meaning of the symptom is now the key, as opposed to suppressing symptoms (Freudian method). Intensify the healing nature of the symptoms and allow for their ultimate release is now the fashion. In essence, the model establishes a safe place to create a virtual trauma that will lead to the true cause of the symptom, which will allow for the quick and total release of the symptom, and all aided by the spiritual inner radar or Voice. The inner radar scans and finds, creates a stream of experiences (dreams, visions, past lives), which are guided by inner healing mechanisms. This model trusts the deeper intelligence that is guiding the process, which is something that the old guard could not bring itself to accept, as evidenced by the never-ending pharmaceutical commercial coming to us through every possible medium.

Grof's holotropic breathwork discoveries spawned more than just pre-natal focus. He saw an even broader spectrum in the transpersonal visions of his patients, transcending time and space, merging boundaries, including all of humanity, mythological experiences, cosmic unity, identification with animals, plant and inorganic life, individual psyche connected with the ultimate totality of existence, with Divinity itself, the Oneness, All-ness and Unity that is so often spoken of by sages and mystics.

These therapeutic discoveries were suggesting that there was something much bigger going on than the healing of an individual's symptoms. Grof seems to have been invited into the energies that were working on healing humanity. It seems to me that some are called to help the healing of individuals and others are called to help the healing of humanity. Stan Grof might have been called to do both, and the tool that he was given was holotropic breathwork (HB). His recognition of it, and his use of it are what make Grof so special.

For centuries shamans and the like have helped guide and heal family tribal units. But people like Stan Grof in breathwork, Jeremy Taylor in dreamwork, Raymond Moody in afterlife work, and Brian Weiss and Michael Newton in past and between life work, have taken the guidance and healing way beyond the tribal unit, to a much larger audience or patient. We should all be deeply appreciative of their time, efforts and devotion to the healing of humanity.

JOURNEY INTO HOLOTROPIC BREATHWORK

Dr. Stanislav Grof's message came from diligent and passionate work that occupied him for several decades of his life. Astonishing messages came in one short morning through the experience of Dr. Jill Bolte Taylor, a noted brain scientist, and a seemingly never-ending week through Dr. Eben Alexander, a noted neurosurgeon. Let us take a quick look and listen to what the Voice brought to or through their powerful experiences before venturing further into the holotropic breathwork trip.

Bolte Taylor's Story

Perhaps I should pass along a few introductory remarks that Dr. Bolte Taylor shared. We might be interested to know that the human genetic code is constructed by the exact same four nucleotides (complex molecules) as every other form of life on the planet, including Earth itself. Next, as members of the human species, we share 99.99% of the same genetic sequence, leaving just 0.01% to account for the significant differences in how we look, think and behave. Regarding the microscopic anatomy of our cerebral cortices, variation is the rule, rather than the exception, contributing to our individual personalities. Sensory information streams in through our sensory systems and is immediately processed through our limbic system. By the time that a message reaches our cerebral cortex for higher thinking, we have already placed a "feeling" upon how we view that stimulation. So, while many of us see ourselves as thinking creatures that feel, biologically and according to Dr. Bolte Taylor, we are feeling creatures that think. Finally, fearful, survival sensations flow quickly through the amygdala to the raging emotional and instinctual side of our left-brain, circumventing the intelligence and cognition of the cerebral cortex. However, when the sensation touches into the intuitive feelings, it reflects the more insightful awareness of the higher cognition that is grounded in the right hemisphere of the cerebral cortex (Bolte Taylor, 1983). Another way that I might put this is that the fearful ego pushes the left-brain buttons of protective animal instincts, while the Higher Self pushes the right-brain buttons of loving spiritual intuitions.

Jill Bolte Taylor's description of her noteworthy morning started with the place that she calls Thetaville, a surreal place of altered consciousness somewhere between dreams and stark reality, where her spirit beamed beautiful, fluid, and free from the confines of normal reality:

Next, I felt a powerful and unusual sense of dissociation roll over me. I felt detached from my normal cognitive functions (*still has some scientist in her speaking*). I seemed to be witnessing my activity as opposed to feeling like the active participant performing the action. Yet I felt as if I was trapped inside the perception of a meditation that I could neither stop nor escape. I was momentarily privy to a precise and experiential understanding of how hard the fifty trillion cells in my brain and body were working in perfect unison to maintain the flexibility and integrity of my physical form. I suddenly felt vulnerable and noticed that the constant brain chatter that routinely familiarized me with my surroundings was no longer a predictable and constant flow of conversation (*Seems to me that we rely on the ego to survey our reality and alert us to the fearful possibilities that might lie ahead.*). As my left-brain chatter began to disintegrate, I felt an odd sense of isolation (*Seems to me that the ego wants us to feel separate from everything and everyone.*) Instead of finding answers and information, I met a growing sense of peace. I felt enfolded by a blanket of tranquil euphoria. As my left hemisphere grew increasingly silent, I was comforted by an expanding sense of grace, as my consciousness soared into an all-knowingness, a "being at one" with the universe. I was aware that I could no longer clearly discern the physical boundaries of where I began and where I ended. I am a sea of water bound inside this membranous pouch. Those little voices, that brain chatter customarily kept me abreast of myself in relation to the world outside of me, were delightfully silent. (*One of the most notable recollections of my enlightening weekend in Santa Monica, which I will speak about later in this writing, was that the ego was noticeably silent and what an ecstatic feeling that silence produced, and still does to this day.).* Although I was compelled by a sense of urgency to orchestrate my rescue, another part of me delighted in the euphoria of my irrationality (*Was the left side still working or was the Voice doing the orchestrating? And, picture the scene of Alistair Sim as Ebenezer Scrooge dancing around his bedroom on the morning of his awakening, and you can imagine what Jill means by euphoria of irrationality.*). I wondered how I could have spent so many years in this body, in this form of life, and never really understood that I was just visiting here. Deep within the absence of earthly temporality, the boundaries of my earthly body dissolved and I melted into the universe. As the dominating fibers of my left hemisphere shut down, they no longer inhibited my right hemisphere, and my perception was free to shift such that my consciousness could embody the tranquility of my right mind (*Perhaps we should capitalize the "m" in mind and recognize how we enable our ego to dominate our perceptions of reality. Does it really take the flooding of the left side of the brain to notice how much we allow the ego to instill such fear in our perceptions of our existence?*) I sat waiting for a wave of clarity that would permit my mind to connect two thoughts together and give me a chance to form an idea, a chance to execute a plan (*Clearly, her linear thinking process was shutting or shut down, and yet she is definitely thinking and expressing the thoughts that were coming to or through her. How is that happening?*). Even though I could hear myself speak clearly within my mind, I realized that I could not speak aloud intelligently. (Bolte Taylor 1983, p. 55)

The Upanishads say that in the unitive state, one sees without seeing for there is nothing separate from him, one hears without hearing for there is nothing separate from him, one tastes without tasting, speaks without speaking, hears without hearing, touches without touching, thinks without thinking and knows without knowing for there is nothing separate from him. Is not this exactly what Jill Bolte Taylor is reporting to us through her experience?

Seems as though the Voice is tuning her into one of the deepest mysteries of human existence. We reside in our bodies, but we are much more than our bodies. We are part of the Oneness of the energy of the universe, of creation, itself. Finally, as Bolte Taylor's morning adventure was coming to its end, the electrical vitality of her molecular mass grew dim, her cognitive mind surrendered its connection to and command over her body's physical mechanics, and with a silent mind and tranquil heart, she felt the enormousness of her energy lift. She clearly understood that she was no longer the choreographer of her life, and said, "In the absence of sight, sound, touch, smell, taste, and fear, I felt my spirit surrender its attachment to this body and I was released from the pain" (Bolte Taylor 1983 p. 63).

Who was writing and delivering the concepts or messages to us? In the stroke description, it clearly was not coming from the mind, as the mind was in disarray, in crisis mode, in collapse; and yet, the witnessing, assessing, and sharing of these events were coming from somewhere. I would say that that somewhere was very important and very transpersonal. To be more specific, there was an observer or witness to the whole series of events that was very much in the room with the body of the scientist, Bolte Taylor. And furthermore, Jill Bolte Taylor did an excellent job of connecting us as readers to the energy of that observer witness, that transpersonal energy that we can readily connect to because that transpersonal energy is *Us*, at our very most transpersonal level, as told to Us by the Voice of Divinity.

ALEXANDER'S STORY

Dr. Eben Alexander, like Dr. Jill Bolte-Talyor, and different from Dr. Stanislav Grof, was not out looking for a message, but surely was delivered one, a very powerful one. What he calls a brush with death and the beyond, his family would call much more than that, as he found himself in a weeklong coma, brought on by an incredibly rare ecoli meningitis. A day or two should have been long enough to totally ravage his brain, but by the Grace of God, he came through without a scratch and happy to tell a most incredible tale. I will say two things that Alexander wanted known. He says that he wrote his book for the scientifically minded skeptics, himself included (pre-coma), to say that what they are so positively sure that they know is flat out wrong. And secondly, that Alexander learned more about human life and purpose in that week when his brain was turned off than in all the years of study and practice combined. These are harsh statements coming from a scientist's scientist.

Alexander's passion, having cheerfully followed in his father's footsteps into neurosurgery and all the dedication and preparation that required, made him a card-carrying member of the scientific community. He graduated from the University of North Carolina at Chapel Hill with a major in chemistry and earned his M.D. at Duke University Medical School. Throughout his eleven years of medical school and residency at Duke as well as Massachusetts General Hospital and Harvard, Alexander focused on neuroendocrinology, the study of the interactions between the nervous system and the endocrine system. He spent two of those years investigating how blood vessels in one area of the brain react pathologically when there is bleeding into it from an aneurysm, what he called a syndrome known as cerebral vasospasm. After completing a fellowship in cerebrovascular neurosurgery in Newcastle-Upon-Tyne in the United Kingdom, Alexander spent fifteen years on the faculty of Harvard Medical School, teaching and operating on countless patients, many of whom had severe and life-threatening brain conditions. I hope we have established that Dr. Alexander knew a thing or two about the science of the workings of the brain. So why such harsh messages to his scientific community?

Let us listen to his words and imagine the Voice that he was experiencing:

I was encountering the reality of a world of consciousness that existed completely free of the limitations of my physical brain. I was in a better-than- average position to judge not only the reality but also the implications of what happened to me. My experience showed me that the death of the body and the brain are not the end of consciousness, and that human experience continues beyond the grave. More importantly, it continues under the gaze of a God who loves and cares about each one of us and about where the universe itself and all the beings within it are ultimately going. (Alexander, 2012, p. 9)

These are not exactly the type of words used by most scientists. They seem to be missing the cold, hard, rigorous facts of the matter. They sound more spiritual than scientific. But, Alexander went on to say,

The place I went was real. It was real in a way that makes life we're living here and now completely dreamlike by comparison. I value life more than I ever did before, because I now see it in its true context. What happened to me in that coma is hands-down the most important story that I will ever tell. But it's a tricky story because it is so foreign to ordinary understanding. At the same time, my conclusions are based on a medical analysis of my experience, and on my familiarity with the most advanced concepts in brain science and consciousness studies. Once I realized the truth behind my journey, I knew I had to tell, and telling it properly has become the chief task of my life. (2012, p. 9)

Well, that moves me, not just because a doctor had a vision and saw the light. It moves me because a doctor and scientist, similar to Dr. Bolte Taylor, sees a reality that is beyond his science training, but still manages to incorporate his science into his understanding of what the Voice said to him in the beyond. In experiencing the Voice, as he did, it completely changed what Alexander sees as his purpose in this lifetime. By the way, Jill Bolte Taylor's book is titled, *My Stroke of Insight* (1983), and Eben Alexander's book is titled, *Proof of Heaven* (2012). Believe me when I tell you that both books are well worth reading.

We need to take a little side trip before heading deeply into holotropic breathwork.

Taking A Side Trip

This side trip was quick and to a very peculiar but powerful location. It is an hour spent in a floatation tank. It was a Father's Day gift from a son and daughter-in-law. They thought that they had given me an hour of relaxing meditation. As you will soon see, they gave me and you a whole lot more than that.

We have all heard the term "out of body experience" (OBE), and while most have not consciously experienced one, we have heard that one leaves the body and sees it there, where it was left. We are thrilled by the notion that what is seeing the left-behind body is not the body, but rather, the inhabitant of the body. This gives us reason to pause and ponder the possibilities.

My experience was not so much seeing the body floating in the tank. It really was much bigger than that. Also, it was not so much about seeing a celestial sight as it was coming to know a deep-seated Truth. The message from the Voice was that we are not the body. It is true that we inhabit it, but we are definitely not it. So, while others have described an "*out* of body experience," I am about to describe a "*not* the body experience."

The combination of pitch-blackness in the tank and the gravity-defying floatation of the body, caused by the heavy concentration of salt, made for some truly insightful impressions. The first came from the awareness that whether my eyes were open or shut, I saw the exact same thing—pure absence of light. Rare it is that eyes shut and eyes open produce the same visual. Some slight light seems to be apparent in one case or the other; but, not in this tank. I opened and shut my eyes a number of times to test this discovery. This condition produced a powerful result, as I saw it, that the body could not tell whether it was awake or asleep. Everyone has seen or experienced when dosing off in a chair, the body seems to jerk. Well, with my eyes wide open and my body definitely awake, the body jerked several times. I remember saying, "Hey body, we are wide-awake here, what gives?"

The floating of the body in body-temperature water resulted in a complete melding of the body with the water, and the effortless floating re-enforced that sensation that I could not tell where the body actually was. I thought that my nasal breathing might provide the clue, but it did not. It seemed as though the exhaled air was a foot or two left of where the nose should have been located, square in the center of my face, if I knew where that was.

Time was clearly irrelevant during this session. There seemed to be a push and pull of exaggerated shortness and longness of time. I remember saying to myself that I have been in here long enough; and yet, I was surprised and startled by the knock on the door, signaling that it was time to leave the tank. It was not that I had fallen asleep, although the body did shift back and forth between conscious and unconscious awareness.

Again, the primary sensation was not *out* of body, but *not* the body, unless I chose to have my mind control it. I found myself in thoughtless moments, and when I would send a thought through, the body would jerk similar to my earlier description.

When the time came to exit the tank, the body and mind required a period of re-adjustment, perhaps similar to what astronauts go through when they return from outer space. Fortunately, there was a showerhead to stand under while everything re-calibrated.

The drives to and from the tank were remarkably different, not physically, but experientially. The drive to the tank was cluttered with traffic and road construction and some anxiety about what was to come. I had experienced some claustrophobic trauma as a child and wondered what it would be like in the closed tank. Turns out that the trauma never came even close to re-appearing. But the same drive home was as peaceful and stress-free as one could possibly imagine. Where cars seemed to be constantly cutting into my lane on the way there, cars seemed to be parting from my lane on the way home. The flow was powerfully noticeable to me.

What I took most away from this experience was the following three conclusions: First, that we are not the bodies and not even the minds, but awareness, consciousness. We may have heard or read these words before, but this session was a way of physically and mentally recognizing this Truth. Second, that we, who inhabit the bodies, are in charge of the bodies. Yes, the bodies seem to run on autopilot much of the time, but perhaps, this is because we allow them to do so. In any event, we must care for our bodies as we would care for our children and of course, as we should care for the living planet where our bodies reside. Third, that we have choices in how we can experience life. The drives to and from the tank were clearly different as a result of my choice to be peaceful or anxious, for my impression of the flow of traffic was remarkably correlated to my state of mind, which, by choice, is totally in my control.

There were three entities in the floatation tank: my body, my mind, and me. All were separate and distinct; yet, all were connected. In considering how the body stays behind when we depart this earthly paradigm and maybe even the mind, but the real energy, that is us, is alive and well. This is what the Voice seemed to be telling me in the floatation tank. One simple hour spent without the use of the five senses allowed me to entertain this powerful message and now share it with you.

ANOTHER SHORT SIDE-TRIP

One more side-trip before holotropic breathwork. This one happened to be a full week in the sacredness of the eco-field of west Texas and in particular with the sacred energies of the Enchanted Rock. I started each day of this week with a short swim followed by a walk around a very simple labyrinth. As a means of tuning myself into this sacred space, I told myself that my intension for this day was to listen from the heart and speak from the heart. I must say that these intensions went a long way towards keeping me firmly planted in the sacred. So, every aspect of the week, from the lectures, the small group discussions, the songs and chants, the sacred practices, the conversations, the meals and the reflections were sacred as could be. However, for me, personally, the biggest intension and by far the most intense moment of the week came on Wednesday. I must say, that I am in no way over this experience. Something inside me says that I am not supposed to be over it, not until I share it with you.

I started the day as I normally did with a quick swim and labyrinth walk. While on the walk, I asked the Divine Feminine to really speak to me today. I said that I really wanted to feel Her presence in my life, not casually, but in such a way that there would be no mistaking it, something truly memorable. Well, as this day unfolded, it became quite clear that something unimaginably sacred was happening to me. We skipped sacred practice and headed straight to Enchanted Rock, a two billion year old, hundred cubic mile hunk of Mother Earth. We formed our circle, sang a song and mystically went out to connect with the Enchanted Rock.

I enjoyed the walk, the beauties of nature, took some pictures and had a peaceful meditation. I stood up to head back to the original gathering place and felt as if I had been struck across my back with a two-by-four. My back ached, my legs trembled, my breath was short, and my energy was gone. I started walking and found myself going from rock to rock, leaning on each for support and rest. I sat down again with my back against a rock and then considered that if I did not get right back up, I might not make it back before the crowd was to head back to the ranch. I stood up and the knowingness came to me that my masculinity would not get me back, that only with the help of the Divine Feminine was I going to make it back. My mind went to work, and I knew that the return trip was not as familiar to me as I had hoped. The markings were in reverse from the way to the meditation spot. Nothing looked as I had expected. So again, the knowingness through the Voice came, "Do not think, just rely on Me, and I will get you back to your group."

Well, I listened, and I walked, and before I knew it, I was back. But my body ached. I felt really beat up. I needed rest but could not find a comfortable position. The group was all around me sharing the beauties of what they had experienced, but I could not join their conversation.

The next two days were physically uncomfortable with aches and pains in places never before felt by me. My mind was scattered as well. My wife's birthday was the following day, and I completely missed calling her to wish her a joyful day. You might say that lots of guys forget their wives special days, that that is what men do. Well, I am not one of those men, and when I realized what I had done, or should I say, had not done, it really hit me hard. Clearly, to me anyway, my mind and body had been traumatized by the powerful connection with the Divine Feminine. Quite simply, I had received what I had asked. I had asked Her to speak loudly and clearly to me, not tap me on the shoulder, and sure enough, I received just what I requested from Her.

The messages coming through Her, while delivered forcefully, were really quite gentle, once I had a chance to reflect. The Voice let me know that She was there for me and was more than willing to respond to my fervent request for conversation with Her. This may well be the main point of this story. Perhaps the Voice is saying that we will be shown, but first we must ask. We must take the initiative to reach out to Divinity in the most reverent way, and we will hear back in the most loving way. This conversation is always available to us. We just have to do a better job of listening, and being more committed to having this Divine conversation, in spite of all the things that we say hinder us in our ways.

Return To Holtropic Breathwork
The time has come to share the trips into holotropic breathwork (HB). There were actually three successive trips, as you will soon see. They came on three successive days.

Day One.
The first trip went as follows: In advance, I purchased the Byron Metcalf compact disc called *The Shaman's Heart II*. It is a seventy-minute journey of tribal-trance drumming and percussion with a continuously built in rhythmic complexity and dynamic intensity. I arranged my spiritual room with my yoga mat and pillow so that I could lie comfortably flat on the floor. I had headphones to hear the music and a blindfold to keep the outside light from my eyes. I had a sketchbook and pastel chalk sticks to do my post HB drawing. In a nutshell, these holotropic breathwork experiences were a means of bypassing the senses, including the mind with the help of the drumming music, creating a trauma through the intentional emptying the body of its oxygen, seeing a vision that ultimately transforms us in some way or another, and drawing this freshly experienced vision so its memory can last some long period of time.

Before entering my spiritual room, I laced on my running shoes and headed to my spiritual hill for some spiritual grounding and uplifting. Having run up and down the hill many times, I was pretty thoroughly exhilarated, came home for a quick shower and headed to my HB session, physically and spiritually ready for anything. Before starting the HB session, I lit shamanic incense, sounded the third eye crystal bowl and centered myself with deep spiritual intentions of letting the shamanic energies in me come forth with a vision that I could share with my spiritual family. These steps were what allowed me or should I say invited me into the very sacred space for communication with the Voice.

Blindfolded and with headset on, I started the music and soon began a long quick series of rather deep exhalations. My body seemed to be emptying out the oxygen, mostly through my mouth and throat, but also through just about every cell of my body. At one point it became clear to me that the oxygen was mostly gone as my mouth was making fish-like movements without any air coming out of it.

Next, I took previously given guidance from my Tai Chi master, to let inhaled air come through the throat, into the back of the head, pass back and forth across the top of the head, and finally be released through the crown. The music seemed to co-operate nicely, as the back and forth movement was in perfect synchronicity with the steady and powerful drumming sounds.

Soon, the body was clearly out of air and did not seem to need it. The music had settled down a bit as well, which allowed me to do my final breathing routine. I took very short breaths and let them wander around for very long moments and exit through the crown. As the air exited through the crown, the whole body trembled and shook like an earthquake or perhaps better, a volcano. There was heat and pressure on the whole left side of my body, through my leg, arm, shoulder and neck. I was not afraid of the feeling, but was certainly well aware of it.

As the music ended, a vision came almost spontaneously. I was paddling a canoe into a glorious sun scene (much more than a sunset). The scene was very dark with a dark blue river, dark green and brown shades of forests on both sides of me and a dark blue sky except for the most radiant vision of a bright yellow center turning into burnt orange, turning into ruby red, turning into deep purple, then joining the sky. All parts of this color spectrum left gently glistening marks on the water in front of me. I would say that it was breathtaking, but I really do not think that I had any more breath to take. This seemed to be a vision from a past life as it reminded me of actual past life scenes that were very similar, only then I was paddling the canoe in the light of day, but, it definitely was the same forest and river, no doubt about that.

I drew and chalked this vision, showed my wife and sat down to write up this report of a most powerful and beautiful experience. I will continue to reflect on this scene; but for now, the most dramatic sense was of a body that did not really need the oxygen and the resulting peaceful, loving state of mind. For the record, this HB work took place about two years prior to the oxygen dream. I do not sense that they were meant to be connected.

DAY TWO.

Day two had all the same preparations as day one, with the hill, the incense, bowl, centering with intention, the blindfold and headphones, yoga mat and pillow. The music began, and I expected to let my breathing stay synchronized with it, but am not so sure that it did. I let the air completely out of the body and allowed it to just lie still until the trembling came. This repeated several times with attempts to experience longer and longer periods of trembling. I am not sure how much the body liked this game, but the mind seemed to enjoy it.

Paleo Butter Chicken

2 teaspoons coconut oil
1 medium onion, diced
4 garlic cloves, minced
1 teaspoon ginger root
½ teaspoon salt
1 teaspoon coriander
1 teaspoon cumin
1 teaspoon cardamom
¼ to ½ teaspoon cayenne pepper (optional)
1 (13.6-ounce) can full-fat coconut milk
1 (6-ounce) can tomato paste
1 pound boneless, skinless chicken breasts or thighs
Juice of 1 lime
¼ cup cilantro, or to taste

In a 10-inch sauté pan over medium heat, heat the coconut oil. Add the onion and sauté until translucent. Add the garlic, ginger, salt and all the spices. Cook 1 minute until fragrant. Stir in the coconut milk and tomato paste until thoroughly combined.

Place the chicken in a slow cooker. Pour the sauce over everything. Cook on high heat for 3 to 4 hours, or on low heat for 6 to 8 hours.

Shred or dice the chicken and return it to the sauce; stir in the lime juice and top with cilantro. Serve with your favorite vegetable, rice or naan bread. Makes 4 to 6 servings.

Recipe courtesy of Costco member Emily Dixon, blogger at Onelovelylife.com.

Shredded Korean Pork

½ cup
(o

Small Wo

Did you know cashews grow on
one nut growing out of each cash

Next, I did a long number of exhalations with little attempt to inhale in between. I did this until the lips got noticeably dry, and then repeated the earlier method of holding still with no air inside, just waiting for the trembling. I alternated these two approaches for the bulk of the musical session. By the end, I was able to hold comfortably for quite a while without air inside. The trembling was just as powerful as the day before, and while the left side of the body felt growing heat and pressure the first time through, the right side had that experience this second time.

A quick vision came during the breathing. It was of an eagle's face directly in front of mine, so that we could see eye to eye. That was powerful, but quick. The longer and stronger vision was of a dark setting with a dark silhouette of a woman walking across the water, in front of an ancient Romanesque arched bridge. She passed by three of the arched segments that were lit up from a golden hue, and then she disappeared. It was as if she was moving in very slow motion and was powerfully mysterious. The woman seemed to be saying something like, "Follow me." There was a confidence in her stride that said, "I know where I am going."

I can say, that physically, the holding without breath was easier this second day, and I was able to hold longer. The tremble was just as strong as the first day. However, like then, it sure seemed that the body did not need air as much as we think that it does. On the spiritual side, both days had a contrasting of an almost eerie darkness with glorious light. There was a gliding solitude in both my canoe motion and in the walking woman. There was silence as the basic backdrop with shimmering water. Both scenes were encased in darkness from all sides. Both scenes had golden light as their centers. In spite of the heaviness of the breathing, I felt calm and peaceful in both scenes. My eyes were tantalized by the shimmering water and by the centering objects of the sun and the women. Neither seemed normal, but both seemed natural at the same time. I was at peace in both moments.

DAY THREE.

To allow comparisons, I used the exact same preparations for the HB experience this third day as in the prior two days; running the spiritual hill (to be clear, it is actually a hill, the hill that kids in town sled down in the winter), incense and crystal bowl for intention setting, centering and calling the shamanic energies, then the blindfold and the headphones. The breathing was again some alternation of many, many exhalations (neighborhood of 200 exhales) with holding the non-breath for some period of time (neighborhood of 200 counts) until the trembling action came on strong. I felt the ability to hold through the trembles longer than the prior days. Also, the time between the exhaling and the trembling was quite calm and peaceful.

I sense that there was a cumulative growth of energy, as this day seemed to create powerful expressions within and outside of me. There were times when the whole house seemed to exhale, as if the house were going to blow apart at the seams, with the incredible force of atomic proportions. There were times when storms seemed to be germinating within and outside of me, which were thunderous and powerful. More than just dark clouds forming, they were more like microbursts of energy that brought black clouds and thunder and ultimately, lightning.

This powerful vision occurred: From a dark empty sky came a stream of translucent large bubbles of light, each one was bright and glistening, with a quivering edge to each bubble and brilliant light inside each one. There was a sense of Divine birthing going on as the bubbles came near and flowed past me. Their pattern was almost as a ferris wheel would push seats towards me and then circle underneath and head back in the direction from which they came. It was continuous until it suddenly ended. I have no idea how long this lasted, I guess, until it was time to tremble and then draw.

This third trip into holotropic breathwork was by far the most extreme in many ways, as the energy of the breathing seemed to be in unison with the house and the universe, for that matter. The energy of the light bubbles, themselves, spoke of Divinity in a most powerful and hard to explain way. The picture that I drew remains vivid in my mind to this day. However, it does not end there. Rather, in the following twelve months, the Voice sent three very visible confirmations of what I had experienced in these HB sessions. The first way came through powerful words in a book that just happened to come into my possession. The words were as follows:

The emanations of radiation from the Cosmos are made up of light and are composed of so-called light bullets that burst forth from the Cosmos…so full of vibrating, pulsating energy, and this energy becomes so condensed that the so-called light bullets are shot out with such radiating force…that element comes to life … Life is the energy that is released by this bombardment of light bullets… This intelligent, emanating energy is God, controlling the universe around us and controlling the universe of our bodies, which are spiritual and not material. (Spalding, 1935. Vol. 3, p. 133)

Believe it or not, I had never read or even considered the concept of orbs of light. I have often thought of the light itself and the loving energy contained in the light. However, I had truly never spent time considering orbs of light.

The second confirmation came in a digital picture that I took during a very spiritually energetic week. All of the pictures that I took during that week were eerily unusual. None of them showed what was in my camera's viewfinder, but became evident once the pictures were already taken. This particular week, for me, was full of early morning labyrinth walking which undoubtedly allowed and invited me into the sacred space. The whole week was very energetic, you might even say painfully energetic. The pictures taken do a good job of revealing this energy. Many of the pictures conveyed energy in a vibratory way, perhaps as a quantum scientist sees atoms as less than solid forms. Some of the pictures were pictures of the planet Jupiter, but displayed a striking lightning-like energy that truly was not in the camera viewfinder.

A friend of a friend (who considers himself a gifted photographer) suggested that these effects were simply a matter of jiggling the camera. He brought a few cameras outside one night to prove that he could replicate the imagery of my pictures. Unfortunately for him, he tried three different cameras, each of greater precision, and found that he was unable to produce my lightning-like shots. He did not seem to understand that the pictures were not about my photography skills; but rather, they were given to me by the Voice to share with you.

One picture really stands out, and that is of a stream of very powerful bullets of light, that I assure you was not in the viewfinder, but was in the resulting picture. There was nothing in the background that could have produced this stream of light bullets, nothing even remotely resembled this stream. But there they were nonetheless. I wondered about these lights and often set this picture side-by-side with my drawing from the third HB session. The combination of the words from the book with the digital picture and the chalk drawing create quite a message for me to consider.

The third confirmation came a couple of months after the passing of a dear elderly friend. Her daughters called me to their mother's house to help them go through her belongings before holding an estate sale to clear most of her things. That day was filled with a mixture of exhilaration and reflections. At one point the girls and I were discussing what should be done with their mother's remains, which they had had cremated and had actually brought the blue box holding her ashes to this day's event.

Shortly after that discussion the girls started dressing up in hats and scarves and canes that their mother had collected. These sixty-something women were really enjoying themselves, engulfed in an almost a child-like energy, and asked me to take pictures on their cameras as memories of this joyful time together, which I gladly agreed to do. A couple of weeks later, one of the daughters sent me one of the pictures from that day. She wanted my take on something that appeared in the picture that certainly was not in the viewfinder when I clicked the camera.

That something was a globe of light, bigger than the box of ashes and positioned right next to the box of ashes. The globe has all the shimmering details of the light bullets from my holotropic breathwork session and the picture taken from the eerie energy week.

Immediately, what came to my mind was that this globe was the woman, mother of these daughters, that I had spent every Thursday with for the five years prior to her passing. She had come to tell her daughters that she was alive and well, had come of her own power and volition, and certainly was not the box of ashes that they had just been discussing. In addition to the globe of light, which was quite large, there were many smaller lights and bubbles that faintly appeared in the picture. I told the girls that their mother must have brought some of her new friends.

Connections

The Voice seemed to be tying all of these concepts together. What Stan Grof, Jill Bolte Taylor and Eben Alexander had experienced and shared, along with the messages of the floatation tank, the Enchanted Rock and the holotropic breathwork sessions, all seemed to be fitting neatly together in this visit from the everlasting and Divine friend of mine. The body, with its magnificent brain, is truly miraculous, but is not who or what we truly are. We inhabit them and care for them, but should not consider them to be our one and only moment in this one and only lifetime. There is a Creator and a power that seems truly bigger and more connected to us than what we have been taught along the way.

Just about everyone mentioned on these sacred trips has seen or heard the Voice and has consciously changed the living purpose of their lives to that of sharing the Voice's message with you and me. What can we do but listen to them and thank them for what they have shared with us. It is up to us to pause and consider deeply what the Voice is saying to us through these special people. Now, having heard the tales of their trips, we can live our lives perhaps differently than we otherwise would have. That has to be a good thing. Don't you think?

THE BUDDHA AND ALTERED STATES

The Buddha seems to have been an "altered states' kind of guy. He certainly advised against accepting the ordinary state of mind with its limitations and suffering, and suggested instead, our fervent search for the enlightened state of nirvana.

From the verse called, "Twin Verses," come these words:

Those whose minds are shaped by selfish thoughts cause misery when they speak or act. Sorrow roll over them as the wheels of a cart roll over the tracks of the bullock that draws it. Those whose minds are shaped by selfless thoughts give joy whenever they speak or act. Joy follows them like a shadow that never leaves them. (Easwaran, 1985, p. 105)

This reminds me an awful lot of my trips to and from the floatation tank. The selfish thoughts causing misery resembles my stressful trip to the tank, while the selfless thoughts giving joy reminds me of the peaceful drive home. In both cases, the choice is definitely ours to be selfish and stressed or selfless and peaceful.

From the verse called, "The Wise," the Buddha states, "If you see someone wise, who can steer you away from the wrong path, follow that person as you would one who can reveal hidden treasures. Only good can come out of it" (Easwaran, 1985, p. 126).

From the verse called, "The Path," Buddha further states, "Pull out every selfish desire as you would an autumn lotus with your hand. Follow the path to nirvana with a guide who knows the way" (Easwaran, 1985, p. 207).

Then the Buddha in the verse called, "The Elephant," advises, "If you find a friend who is good, wise, and loving, walk with him all the way and overcome all dangers" (Easwaran, 1985, p. 224). All three of these strike me as the dark woman crossing the water in front of the Romanesque arched bridge. She had a soothing, silent message that exuded confidence and sense of knowing direction. I felt as comfortable as it seems that the Buddha wants us to feel when we have right direction being offered to us. The Voice is that direction in my life.

From the verse called, "Pleasure" comes this guidance: "If you long to know what is hard to know and can resist the temptations of the world, you will cross the river of life" (Easwaran, 1985, p. 184). I feel these powerful words as I reflect on my paddling the river past the dark forests and heading towards the vibrant sun scene. There was much more than a sunset that I was heading towards. The feeling of crossing the river of life was definitely an aspect of the shimmering colors on the water.

CHAPTER 4

Questing for a Vision

▲ ▲ ▲

MY VISION QUEST WAS REALLY a fifteen-month experience, always in the most sacred of spaces and clearly guided and encouraged by the Voice. There are many forms of vision questing and mine was patterned after the sacred quests of Native Americans.

DEFINITION OF A VISION QUEST

As we get started, it might be helpful if we ask "What is a vision quest?" A vision quest, according to Webster's dictionary and me, is a supernatural experience in which an individual interacts with a guardian spirit or higher energy to obtain advice, direction, protection, or meaning and purpose in life. Of particular importance to indigenous North and South American peoples, these rituals varied by tribe. Generally, vision quests require extensive preparation; occur over a period of several days; involve solitary vigils, preferably in the wilds of nature; encounter some form of crisis; and are accentuated by devout prayer and fasting.

The vision quest, beyond just the Americas, is said to be one of the most universal and ancient means of finding spiritual guidance and deep understanding of one's life purpose. All of the great avatars of all the great faiths have been known to head out into the wilderness to interrupt their human experiences for doses of Divine inspiration. Common to success in vision questing, in my view, is total surrender to the Higher Energy of the sacred and holding extremely humble and devout intentions.

The Lakota Sioux word for vision quest translates to "crying for a dream," because the vision quester, both physically and spiritually, cries out for a vision or sacred dream. These words are truly meant to convey the passion of the vision quester, to hearing and seeing what the Voice wants to show and tell. The vision quest is also often called "going up the hill," because the vision quester often goes to a nearby mountain or hilltop to have his or her experience. Ideally, the quest is completed deep in nature, far away from civilization, at a meaningful location chosen by the quester.

A Spiritual Guide

Because of the powers inherent in the experience and the wilds of the selected location, the vision quester is carefully guided, aided, and instructed in all preparations by a Medicine Person, a Holy Person.

Upon completion, the vision quester is brought back to camp to share his or her experience with the holy person, who provides spiritual guidance and interpretation, and ways to better understand the full meaning of the vision. The relationship between the vision quester and the holy person must be built upon unconditional love and trust.

Examples Of A Vision

Two well-known vision quests of the Lakota tradition came through Crazy Horse and Lame Deer. Although most white Americans think of Crazy Horse as the fearless warrior, both of these men were known in the eyes of their own people as extremely holy men.

Vision Of Crazy Horse.

Taken from Joseph Marshall's *The Journey of Crazy Horse* came a description of Crazy Horse's original and most powerful vision:

From a small, still lake, bursting upward from the blue calmness, a horse and its rider broke through the surface and rode across the land. A lightning mark was painted across one side of the man's face, and on his bare chest were blue hailstones. Behind them was a dark rolling cloud rising higher and higher, bringing deep rumbling thunder and flashes of lightning. The horse, strong and swift, changed colors through red, yellow, black, white and blue. Arrows filled the air but none touched this man or horse. Just above them flew a red-tailed hawk. People of his own kind suddenly rose up all around them, grabbing the man and pulling him down from behind. (Marshal, 2004, p.71)

Those who know the Crazy Horse life story, know that he seemed more than just gifted in battle, but impenetrable by arrows and bullets. Also, his ultimate death was affected not actually by the whites, but by jealous red men who were envious of his reputation. So, the vision provided a very mixed blessing of courage in battle but a betrayal in the end. Incidentally, the name Crazy Horse was not to imply that either he or his horse was crazy. Nor did it come from or through his vision quest. Rather, it was honorably handed down to him from his holy man father as was his from holy man grandfather. In white man's terms, he might have been Crazy Horse III.

Vision Of Lame Deer.

Lame Deer, a Sioux medicine man, born roughly twenty-five years after Crazy Horse's passing, came from an even longer line of holy men. In fact, it was through his original and most powerful vision quest that he learned that he would carry on the family tradition of medicine men. Taken from *Lame Deer, Seeker of Visions*, written by Lame Deer with help of Richard Erdoes, we were given these descriptions:

Darkness had fallen upon the hill. Blackness was wrapped around me like a velvet cloth. It made me listen to the voices within me. I thought of my forefathers who had crouched on this hill before me, over the past two hundred years. I could sense their presence right through the earth. Sounds came to me through the darkness. Suddenly I felt an overwhelming presence, as if a very large bird were sharing these very tight quarters. His cries were near and far at the same time. I was so frightened that I shook the rattle and grabbed and held tight the sacred pipe. A voice said to me, "You are sacrificing yourself here to be a medicine man. A man's life is short, make yours a worthy one." I then saw my great-grandfather and knew instantly that he wanted me to take his name. I knew that I was to be a *wicasa wakan*, a medicine man. (1994, p. 5)

PREPARATION FOR A PERSONAL VISION QUEST

My own vision quest began the moment that I drove my stake into the ground, in ceremony, some fifteen months prior to my actual time in the mountains of Santa Cruz. These fifteen months were spent preparing myself for this very sacred quest for a vision.

What does it mean to prepare for a vision quest? To answer this question, it was extremely important that I began to get to know and honor the vision questing ways of Native Americans of old. To this end, I read books by or about Crazy Horse, Black Elk, Lame Deer and my vision questing mentor, Will Taegel.

These special men of the nineteen, twenty and twenty first centuries, live or lived their lives in accordance with the sacred ways of the Native Americans, and carry the sacred meaning of this sacred ritual to us. These men spoke of the sacred symbols of the Native American cultures. Will Taegel, a modern day shaman, spoke of the truly historical significance of the conch shell, which constitutes one of the earliest indications of expanding human consciousness beyond practical survival into metaphoric and symbolic meaning. Black Elk spoke of the *chanupa* (sacred pipe) that he learned to rely on as his spirit guide, as it led him to the medicines, waterholes and shelters of his lifetime. Lame Deer insisted that "the earth, the rocks, the minerals, are very much alive," and he implored us to "talk to the rivers, to the lakes, to the winds and to our relatives" (Lame Deer, 1994, p. 108).

All of these men spoke of the importance of the purification that goes on within the sweat lodge, a practice that precedes every important Native American ceremony, most certainly including the vision quest. I partook in the sweat lodge purification prior to heading out to my vision quest, but more importantly, I spent the six months leading up to the quest in my own form of spiritual purification. I called it "restoring the temple," and it was my way of purifying my body, mind and spirit so that the Light of Divinity could shine with clarity and brilliance, for all to see. During the six months preceding the quest, I flushed away toxins, I burned away excess fat, I added physical and mental strength, and I devoted myself to honoring the Divine in me. Sure, I changed my food intake and my exercise regiments, but those were just the implements of the spiritual intentions that I had set for myself. With the purest of intentions, the much-improved physicality manifested accordingly, not the other way around. I ran a hill each morning and held in mind the energies of the directions as the Native Americans have honored: north, east, south, west, earth (grandmother), sky (grandfather), ancestors and relations. I ended each session with the words *mitakuye o'yasin*, meaning all my relations, and reminding me that every living thing is truly and Divinely related as One.

There was a strong, elderly tree at the base of my hill, which I got to know quite well. It guarded the hill and the pond behind it. A turtle from the pond laid her eggs right along the path that my footsteps made up the hill. Children visiting the swing sets near the hill watched and then followed my example of climbing and enjoying the hilltop. Clearly, this was a sacred place, unbeknownst to most people living in this town. I am reminded of Lame Deer's advice to be one with the land.

I tied a string of 405 spiritual bundles (prayer ties) into a thirty-foot diameter circle. This circle would protect me in the wild of the vision quest. These bundles were cut from colored cotton cloth, each color representing the directional energies. Red was for north, yellow for east, white for south, black for west, green for earth, blue for sky, a misty purple (my selection) for ancestors and a patchwork (again, my selection) was for relations. I filled each bundle with a pinch of either sage, tobacco, lavender or hand-ground dark chocolate. Together they smelled divine. The tying of these bundles took many days, but I was in no hurry. I set up a sacred workspace and listened to Native American music as I prayed into each bundle. Thus, during my time in the quest forest, I would be surrounded by these 405 heartfelt prayers, bringing me safety, comfort and a vision to share when I returned. Some say that we are to cry for a vision, I guess that I prayed for one instead.

So far, I have driven the stake into the ground, setting my intention to quest; I have acquainted myself with Native American culture and traditions; I have acquired my sacred pipe; I have tied my circle of 405 spiritual bundles; and I have purified my body, mind and spirit for this quest. The only preparation left to speak of is the crisis that is needed to create the vision that is to appear.

CREATING A CRISIS

In olden times, a Native American boy was left in a secluded piece of land for usually four days and nights of fasting, sleep deprivation and prayer, creating a crisis, which helped to bring forth his vision, leading him into adulthood, a true rite of passage. I was only going to be out there, fasting and praying, for one day and night, so I felt that I needed to do something that would supercharge this experience and help create the crisis. I chose to begin my fast several days beforehand, so that I would at least arrive weakened by my hunger.

The night before my quest was spent signing and dancing Native American songs around a ceremonial campfire. Powerful spiritual energies bubbled up inside of me.

THE PHYSICAL QUEST ITSELF

The quest day began with the purifying sweat lodge ritual. The lodge was filled with vision questers and accompanying supporters. Each supporter directly addressed his or her quester with words of strength and encouragement, particularly addressed to the quester's vulnerability. When my supporter's turn came, he said the most interesting thing. He said, "Lighten up Tom. You need to go into the quest joyfully and full of humor. So, don't be so serious." Well, this was not the first time that I have been given this advice, and I knew that it was coming straight from his heart, so I took it with me to my quest site with a great deal of respect.

VISION QUEST SITE.

I should probably take a moment to describe my setting in the forest. The trail that I took from campsite to my quest site was a long ways away, ending at a descending path from about fifty feet above my landing spot. Near the landing spot was a subtle wooden staircase that descended to a flat circular ground about thirty feet in diameter. At the center of this natural circle were seven majestic redwoods, all tightly clustered together. At the edge between the flat ground circle and the forest itself were long redwood logs. They served as a border between my circle and the dense forest, holding the circle, so to speak. Next to the seven redwoods was a small wooden bench, made from a log, about four feet long, cut through the middle, forming a flat surface. From the center of my circle, and looking up panoramically, was a hill-like climb of about fifty or sixty feet. This view of the forest reminded me of the Greco-Roman amphitheaters of ancient times or the rising seats of modern day musical venues. So, let me summarize this setting: from an elevated trail came a descent of about fifty feet to a log-bordered flat ground circle with seven stately redwoods clustered in its center, and a wooden bench. This is where I spent the next twenty-seven hours in sacred vision quest.

EXPERIENCES ON MY QUEST.

Pretty early on in my quest I found myself sitting on the ground, my back up against a tree, listening to what I first thought was a bird singing to me. I strained my eyes to see where this sound was coming from. High up a tree was not a bird, but a squirrel, and it was not singing, it was laughing—yes, laughing! I immediately thought of the advice that my supporter had given me. This squirrel was laughing up a storm of laughter in me. It stayed up there for close to an hour, or until I was probably all laughed out.

Next came a parade of clouds through the tops of the redwoods, with outlines of humans and animals in all shapes and sizes. It brought back joyful, childhood memories of the Thanksgiving Day parades. Jesus and the Buddha and many spiritual teachers, healers and and guides of all faiths seemed to float on by. Where the squirrel had tickled my funny bone, these awesome clouds had grabbed my attention in a most reverent and humble way.

At dusk, my eyes seemed to be playing tricks on me. Gazing up one of the hills, what appeared was a group of joyful animals hopping around with incredible playfulness. It was pleasant and a bit eerie at the same time. The next morning I was able to notice the large rocks that had come to life as these joyful friends. I am reminded again of Lame Deer's advice.

Once the sun went down, it was dark, very dark. The tops of the trees folded over each other in such a way as to block the view of most of the stars and totally block the light of the moon. So, all possibilities of natural light were removed from my scene, leaving it pitch black. I had held in my mind that I would not sleep through the upcoming vision. At around two or three in the morning I was lying on the four-foot bench in a bit of a fog, somewhere between awake and asleep. Suddenly, I noticed myself rolling off the bench onto a large, sharply pointed rock. The fall left a mark, but more importantly, landing on the sharp stone left me, from that moment absolutely, positively awake and alert. I realized that I was cold, so, I put on my hooded sweatshirt and tied it tight, which completely removed my peripheral vision (as if I could see in the utter darkness of the night). But there I sat, stone sober awake and said to myself, "I am not hungry; I am not tired, and I am not frightened here in this forest, so from where will the crisis come that is going to produce the vision of this quest?

Well, not ten minutes later I heard the sound of an approaching animal. My first thought was, "I wonder if it is the two deer that I saw the day before, coming to visit me." Without my eyesight, my ears were working extra hard, and it became clear to me that it was not the sound of deer that I was hearing. The animal was big and strong and lower to the ground than a deer. Not only could I here the thump, thump, thump of its gait, but I could feel its presence coming towards me. From its presence, I knew that it was not the least bit afraid of me. This was its forest, and I was its visitor, not the other way around. I could feel the presence of a hundred plus pound animal coming up the hill, from the other side of the redwood logs, circling behind the cluster of redwoods, and approaching me from over my left shoulder. When it came to just a couple of feet away, I noticed that I was not afraid, but thought that this night I would either live or die. What else was there? Escape up the inclined walls of the forest amphitheater was not a possibility, so, there I was.

Suddenly, a most spectacular, powerful energy arose inside of me. It was a power beyond anything that I had ever felt before as a human being. It seemed to encircle me with this power like a protective shield. But I did not actually need protection, and this power had a Voice. I saw that it connected me with the animal, and if I were to translate the Voice into words, they would go something like this, "Friend, that is close enough. Sit a while and let us talk." The next thing I noticed was that the animal stopped just a foot away from me, at the edge of my bench, and sat down. Time is strange at times like these, so I am not sure how long this surreal energy exchange took place. There was a mystical conversation going on between the animal and me. In visual terms, it looked like the bubble captions of a comic strip, but without the written words. Eventually, the animal stood up, backed up and walked down the hill the same way that it had come up the hill earlier.

Sharing The Vision.

While this experience left a lasting memory in my mind, what went on from this moment until I returned to camp, many hours later, is mostly a blank sheet. I know that I walked the circle in prayer. I sense that I was anxious to return to the campsite. I know that I did not sleep. Eventually, the time came for me to return to camp to share my vision with Will Taegel, my holy man. With excitement and tears I shared all that I had experienced. Again, how much time this took is hard to know. But when I was through telling my tale, I felt completely spent. I returned to my cabin, called my wife, and then hit the pillow for some much needed sleep.

The next morning, all the vision questers and supporters gathered as a group to share our tales. I thought that I aught to know what kind of animal had been with me, so I went to the internet and googled "the animals of the Santa Cruz Mountains." The first item that came up was the picture of a mountain lion and a caption that read, "4,000 mountain lions roam the mountains of Santa Cruz." So there is that. We gathered and shared our stories. Laughter, tears and amazement filled the air as each of us offered powerful moments for others to hear, enjoy and appreciate. It was a Divinely orchestrated show and tell.

The Naming Ceremony.

Next, in Native American tradition, it was customary to be given a new name that honors the events of the vision quest and allows a sense of direction as we march forward into our new lives. Most names given were nature-based names like "Two Trees Standing," or "Deer By The Brook," or "Eagle Landing." You follow my drift. As I told my tale, still in a bit of a fog, I noticed waves of laughter and tears and more laughter and astonishment and again tears, but when Will Taegel proclaimed my name, I nearly fell off my feet. He said that I had come to the end of the path and my new name would be "Divine Power Speaks."

Teachings Of The Quest

I will leave you to interpret for yourselves what this all means to you, but there were two very powerful meanings that came through to me in the very name that the Voice gave me through Will Taegel. Prior to this vision quest, my deepest understandings of Divinity, the Creator, and what it is to be a Child of God were all known to me experientially and later supported by readings and teachings. All through this vision questing preparation I kept hearing from the Voice, "We are One. We are Love. We are Power." This was so different from all the years and lifetimes of hearing from organized religions how separate we are from God. The Voice seemed to be flushing these limiting thoughts down the proverbial toilet. Instead, coming to me was a deeply profound concept: Oneness with Divinity with Love and with Power.

Some very interesting words had come to me through what I call the White Book. Actually, it is from Baird T. Spalding and is called, *Life and Teaching of the Masters of the Far East*. From this book came the following:

Man always questions the nature of beginning. It is not easy to conceive of anything without its origin. As far as man is concerned, beginning came into being with conscious or separate identity. But before man is spirit, and that state is one to which we return. That God is in no way the form of human being, but God is that Supreme Intelligent Energy that permeates every form and every atom of the universe, including man. And when you realize that Supreme Intelligent Energy is fully centralized within your human form, you are that Power, and by fully acknowledging that this Power acts through you, you are that Power. That each and every individual has the ability to be that Power. That is the Kingdom of God into which every individual is born, as soon as all see and know this, all are of God's Kingdom. (1955, Vol. 5, p. 44,)

When the Power of these words and the Power of this vision was matched up with the name given, "Divine Power Speaks," well, you can imagine what energy flowed through me at the particular moment.

The second reason that the given name hit me so hard, in a good way, was that the Native American tradition is not big on using the term Divine. Sure, there is Great Spirit and other names for honoring the Creator's energy, but Divine did not seem to be in its vocabulary. So, when Will Taegel, an authentic Native American Holy Man, uttered this word at such an important moment, it really said to me, "We get you, and we get your message. We have crossed a boundary here. We have melded together two very important and seemingly different spiritual schema, and if these two spiritual borders can be removed, then why not all spiritual borders?"

This does not mean to diminish the honoring of individual spiritual belief systems, but it does suggest that co-existence is more than just a bumper sticker.

Tribal Connections Of A Quest

There was tremendous energy in the camp after the stories were told. Vision questers and supporters were in feverish conversation. One supporter approached me to say that just before falling off to sleep on the night of the quest, she had a vision of me sitting with a very large black cat, a jaguar or puma, she thought. She said that she hoped that I would not look it in the eyes, as that would have invited immense trouble for me. I jokingly asked if she had considered sending someone up to warn me, but we know that she did not really need to do that, did she? Interesting stuff, but there is more. Six months later I learned more of what this friend had seen in her vision that night. She said that I was wearing a hooded sweat-shirt and could not make out my face because my back was to her. My friend said that I was sitting on a bench with a sharp stone underneath. She said that she saw the particles of the animal's breath and my own breath came together in a mystical way, like two little clouds coming together as one. My friend said that she was very moved by the experience of her vision contained inside my vision. And, so am I.

Concluding Thoughts

Looking back, I notice the Voice in every aspect of this powerful story. I notice the Voice in the wisdom that was shared by or though Crazy Horse, Lame Deer, Black Elk and Will Taegel. I notice the Voice in every moment of my vision quest preparation, from the inspiration that I felt to put my stake in the ground, through every prayer bundle that I tied, through every step up and down my hill and other aspects in the ways of my purification of body, mind and spirit, through every song that I sang or danced, through every bite of food that I did not eat during the days leading up to and including the quest, through every powerful moment of the quest, with the squirrel and the cloud figures and the animated, playful animals and most importantly, through the mountain lion interaction, through the overlapping and confirming vision of my supporter friend, and finally, through the sacred name given to me at the end by my holy person. Every single step along the way seemed to be guided and encouraged by the Voice, leading me through inspiration, dedication, purification, collaboration, and finally, through appreciation for all that was presented to or through me. All that is meant to be presented to or through me in the many years to come, as my new name suggests, "Divine Power Speaks!!"

MOMENTS TO QUEST WITH THE BUDDHA

The Buddha certainly lived the most significant moments of His life as a vision quester. He was known to discard all of the luxuries of life and set out to meditate deeply until he found his purpose in life. He then most generously shared his interpretations of what he had discovered on his Divine quest. Several meaningful questing quotes popped up in the verses of The Dhammapada. The following are just a few:

From the verse called "Mind," is stated, "Remember, this body is like a fragile clay pot. Make your mind a fortress and conquer Mara with the weapon of wisdom. Guard your conquest always. Remember that this body will soon lie in the earth without life, without value, useless as a burned log" (Easwaran, 1985, p.116). The purification and preparations for my vision quest come through these words from the Buddha. It takes dedication and effort to overcome the affects of Mara and finding lasting peace. His last line suggests to me that there is no time to waste, so keep moving.

From the verse called, "The Saint," we are called to wisdom,

Wisdom has stilled their minds, and their thoughts, words, and deeds are filled with peace. Freed from illusion and from personal ties, they have renounced the world of appearance to find reality. Thus have they reached the highest. They make holy wherever they dwell, in village or forest, on land or at sea. With their senses at peace and minds full of joy, they make the forest holy. (Easwaran, 1985, p. 134)

My moment in the forest of the Santa Cruz Mountains was clearly holy to the mountain lion and me. Together, we had overcome appearances and found the reality of the Power that flowed to and through us as One.

From the verse called, "Punishment," comes this thought, "Those whose mind is serene and chaste, whose senses are controlled and whose life is non-violent — these are true Brahmins, true monks, even if they wear fine clothes" (Easwaran, 1985, p. 144). The purification was so real and the non-violence between the mountain lion and me was so natural, that peace and serenity were all that mattered during that mystical moment.

From the verse called, "Anger," wisdom is revealed, "Injuring no one, self-controlled, the wise enter the state of peace beyond all sorrow. Those who are vigilant, who train their minds day and night and strive continually for nirvana, enter the state of peace beyond all selfish passions" (Easwaran, 1985, p. 188). Clearly, again, the mountain lion and I were One in this mystical moment given to us by the Voice.

From the verse called "Impurity," we reflect on the journey,

Your life has come to an end, and you are in the presence of death. There is no place to rest on this journey, and you are so unprepared. Light the lamp within; strive hard to attain wisdom. Become pure and innocent, and you will be free from birth and death. (Easwaran, 1985,   p. 194)

As Will Taegel uttered to me, "You have come to the end of your path." Yet my life had truly just begun. The lamp was truly lit and the wisdom was flowing freely. "Surrender," says the Voice, "and discover that you are free!!"

From the verse called, Varied Verses, we rejoice,

The disciples of Guatama are wide awake and vigilant, with their thoughts fo-
cused on the Buddha day and night...absorbed in dharma day and night...with
their thoughts focused on sangha day and night...with their thoughts focused on
sense-training day and night...rejoicing in compassion day and night...rejoicing
in meditation day and night.
(Easwaran, 1985, p. 212)

Just before the mystical moment in the forest of the Santa Cruz Mountains, I knew that I was
awake and vigilant. I was focused on hearing and seeing what the Voice had for me. It did not take
long before the presentation began. I definitely rejoiced with the news from the Voice. The Power that
I had been searching for, not as a weapon, but as a connection with my Creator, was there to be wit-
nessed not only by the lion and me, but also through the dream or vision of the supporter in camp.
From the verse called, the "Bhikshu," we learn,

Train your eyes and ears; train your nose and tongue. The senses are good friends
when they are trained. Train your body in deeds, train you tongue in words, train
your mind in thoughts. This training will take you beyond sorrow. (Easwaran,
1985, p. 244)

In the darkness of that night, my ears were working extra hard. My senses truly knew
what was coming up the hill and into my circle. The cluster of seven mighty redwoods was
my sanctuary, and the bench was my altar. The Power was in the bubble of communication
between the lion and me. The training was complete, and the peace was between us.

CHAPTER 5

Adventures in the Afterlife

▲ ▲ ▲

WE ARE ABOUT TO EMBARK on sacred adventures that I took into the afterlife. We will examine for ourselves this mystical perception and come away with our own views on life and living, here, there and everywhere, or more precisely *forever*. I can assure you that the Voice has something very definitely worth hearing on this score.

Is there life after death? That is a big question. Neanderthal men, one hundred thousand years ago, are said to have buried their dead in biers of flowers, perhaps indicating that they saw death as an occasion for celebration, as if to celebrate a transition from this world to the next. More recently, the Greeks of 500 to 400 B.C. were talking and writing about this question, and caught the attention of one, Raymond Moody, a young philosophy scholar at the University of Virginia in the late 1960s.

At age 24, this young man knew more about ancient Greek philosophy than most natural born Greeks of any age. But of all the possible Greek philosophical concepts with which Moody acquainted himself, the one that truly captured his attention was the concept of life after death. In a Divine way, people began approaching Moody with story after story of their personal experiences near death, now commonly known as near-death experience (NDE). Raymond

Moody chronicled these many stories and quickly became the first known author and authoritarian on the topic of near-death experience, at least in modern times.

YEARNING FOR AN AFTERLIFE

In a seemingly unrelated thought, I grew up in the sixties and seventies and as a result was a big fan of the Beatles: John, Paul, George and Ringo. Clearly, their music caught on, and each became a notable figure in his own right. John was the activist, Paul wrote love songs, Ringo was the odd one with the beautiful wife, and George was the quiet one. John and Paul, who received most of the world's attention, wrote most of the early songs. However, the last album had the spiritual influence of George, who I would say, was anything but quiet.

George had a lot to say and do and thanks to a documentary called, *George Harrison, living in the material world,* by Martin Scorsese, I came to know the spiritual side of George that stretched well beyond his popular music. Of particular interest to me was George's life long dedication to perfecting, for himself, the moment of passing from this life. He desperately wanted to grab hold of God's hand in the purest way possible, and thus, diligently prepared for this moment through his prayerful living, his deep meditation, his soulful music and his unconditional service to humanity.

I remember George Harrison wrote so eloquently in his song, "My Sweet Lord," these words, "I really want to see you, really want to be with you, really want to know you, really want to show you, but it takes so long, my Lord." His longing for the final destination, and his understanding that it would be a most Divine homecoming and connection with God is clear to me in his words.

THE GREEKS AND THE AFTERLIFE

Let us take a quick run through the ancients of Greece to note what they had to say about the afterlife.

In pre-philosophic times there were rhapsodies, purifiers, air-walkers, revenants, out of body travelers, underworld journeyers, oracles, prophet doctors and dead evokers. All came well before Pythagoras (mostly known to us non-Greek "geeks" for his mathematical discoveries). But Pythagoras was a very "out there" man in his own right. He was a coiner of the concept of "friendship" when most were driven by "kinship." He sought the knowledge of the oracles of the dead and loved music. Pythagoras valued the feminine (doesn't the world still seems challenged), introduced reincarnation and created the very first institution of higher education.

Parmenides was the very first to offer logical deduction and showed his students ways to experience rather than just learn about or memorize.

Heraclitus spoke on many topics but can be remembered for suggesting that the revenants watch over the living and the dead, what we now might consider guardian angels.

Xenophanes pioneered the concept of epistemology, how do we know what we know, as well as techniques for acquiring knowledge.

Democritus shared his perception of the geometric point having no dimension, what is now a deep concept being worked on currently by noted quantum physicists.

Anaxagoras came just before Socrates and shared his view of holographic theory of matter, where we are made of a little bit of everything. I imagine that he was speaking physically, but I often wonder if this might not be true spiritually. I am a firm believer in past lives, for I have seen many and have guided many through their own. While I do not sense that I was John the Baptist or

Saint Francis of Assisi, I cannot help thinking that there is a bit of both of them in me.

Socrates and Plato had much to share on the topic of life after death. In Plato's *Phaedo*, Raymond sees the gold standard of inquiry into the rational approach to the key questions concerning life after death. Is there life after death? Is there a soul that survives in lieu of the body that does not? This glorious piece of writing shares the last hours spent by Socrates and his closest students as they examine what would become of Socrates after his imminent execution. Phaedo, the witness and narrator of the story starts by declaring that he had a singular feeling at being in Socrates' company at the time of his death. He said that he died so fearlessly, so noble and gracious. Phaedo said that Socrates appeared blessed with a Divine call, and that he would arrive happy, if any man ever was when he arrived there (Jowett, 2008, p. 47).

From this same writing, Socrates shared that "at the time of death, he was going to gods who were wise and good, and to departed men who are better than those that he left behind" (Jowett, 2008, p.52). Socrates felt that the real philosopher has reason to be of good cheer when he is about to die, and after death he may hope to obtain the greatest good in the other world. Furthermore, "of the true votary of philosophy, he is always pursuing death and dying, he has had the desire of death, all his life long" (Jowett, 2008, p. 53). Furthermore, Socrates spoke of the "true philosophers," as follows: "During my whole life, I have been seeking, according to my ability, to find a place, whether I have sought in a right way or not, and whether I have succeeded or not, I shall truly know in a little while, God willing, when I myself arrive in the other world— such is my belief" (Jowett, 2008, p. 59).

Socrates' favorite doctrine, according to his friend and student Celeb, was that knowledge is simply recollection, necessarily implying a previous time in which we learned that which we now recollect. This would also suggest that our soul had been some place before existing in the form of man, which constituted a portion of Socrates' proof of the soul's immortality. Taken even further with regard to absolute essence recollection are these words from Socrates,

When we see something material that we know does not match perfectly to absolute essence, implies that we have seen and recollect absolute essence before we have seen the material. That is, our soul is aware before our physical birth what absolute is…enough so that our human senses know that they are seeing a look-a-like, not an original. (Jowett, 2008, p. 66)

George Harrison, mentioned before, wrote a whole album of songs about "living in the material world" and how unreal it actually is. He noted that nothing, including his wife, his money, his home, or any of his so-called possessions were real or his, that the only real thing that truly mattered was God and one's connection to God. Harrison spoke openly that ignorance was all that kept us from seeing and knowing what was real, and that ignorance was to blame for our habit of separating our perception from true essence. Raymond Moody may assist in the overcoming of our ignorance with his studies.

Near-Death Experiences

As mentioned earlier, when Raymond became bitten by the life after death "bug," he was immediately bombarded with first-hand cases of near-death experiences (NDE). Let us take a moment to acquaint ourselves with the basic characteristics of NDE, as voiced first by Raymond and then by so many others. It is called near-death experience because the person relating the experience had actually been declared dead by doctors, nurses, paramedics, etc. Their hearts stopped, or their brain activity stopped, or they were in a comatose state for some required period of time to warrant the death declaration. So, let us just agree that they were dead. Clearly, if they reported these experiences, then they, in fact, must have come back to life – amazing! What was clearly of interest to Raymond Moody and others was what the persons reported having happened while they were dead. And to be sure, what they reported was repeated time and time again, producing a clear-cut set of characteristics.

Some or all of these characteristics have been reported to Moody in every case. Ineffably, hearing the news of their supposed death, feelings of peace, far off sounds, dark tunnel, out of body, spiritual body (cloud, smoke-like, vapor, transparent, wispy, energy), absence of limitations (space, time, matter), clear-headed, direct thought transfer, meeting others (guides, deceased loved ones), the Light (Christ, angels, guides, emissaries), truth, acceptance, the review of their life (vivid, real, three-dimensional, series of pictures or slides), the border line, coming back (whether or not one wanted to), certainty of its reality, effects on lives (renewed determination, new moral principles, seeking knowledge), and finally, the fear of death is gone. What an amazing assortment of feelings to experience. What was Raymond Moody or others to do with this incredible information?

Well, one thing that Moody said "right off the bat" was that he was not going to try to prove the existence of life after death. What he was going to do was to continue his inquiry into the concept. He did so for the next forty years, reading, studying, and continuing to collect first-hand accounts and more. Moody approached his inquiry along the lines of what he considered disciplined reason rather than through faith or experience (*He really had neither on which to fall back.*), which Moody considers to be spiritual discipline.

As a side note, the skeptics of ancient Greece developed the practice of continuing the inquiry without drawing conclusions, the perpetual searching, so to speak. Today's skeptics are not nearly as authentic as they consider themselves to be. It is not that they do not come to a conclusion, but rather, they come to the conclusion that they do not believe the given thought.

Raymond Moody is a true skeptic in the authentic sense of the word. His whole life has been in pursuit of truth, without actually concluding what the conclusions were, which is a big part of his true humility, and is closely related to how Plato spoke of Socrates. While being considered the world's authority on NDE, it was not until quite recently that he actually leaned in one direction or the other. Moody now leans toward believing in life after death, where the arrows of NDE are clearly pointing.

The ultimate scientific skeptic argues that it is the physical nature of being so near death that causes the beatific experiences that have been reported. In other words, the lack of oxygen to the brain, the effects of heart stoppage, the trauma and other clearly medical phenomenon, which make the brain do what it does in these experiences. Well, Raymond has an answer to these scientific skeptics, and it is a really powerful answer.

Along the way, people started approaching Moody with stories of first-hand experiences of these same beatific happenings to them, but these were not people who were near death, but rather, people who had been sitting with dying loved ones. His book entitled, *Glimpses of Eternity, Sharing a Loved One's Passage From This Life To The Next* (2010), was loaded with moving stories of doctors', nurses', caregivers' and family members' accounts of what they experienced while comforting loved ones just prior to death. Moody labeled these experiences, shared death experiences (SDE), and here are notable characteristics: room changing shape, mystical light, being swept up in a cloud, electrical sensations, hearing beautiful music, joint review of loved one's life (which was the most incredible to Raymond), predictive experiences. (*Someone not yet known to be dead arrives on the celestial scene, and is later learned to have passed away just at the correct time.*) People would say that they felt like they had left the physical body and went into another plane with her or him.

The ultimate answer to the scientific-minded skeptics who were disbeliev-ing in NDE was that these SDE people were not even close to their own death; and yet, they experienced such overlapping moments with the dying. These moments deeply moved the SDEs in ways similar to the NDEs. They often said that it changed my life, and the lives of each of us who were with her or him at the end to witness the pure joy of what they called "going home."

Raymond Moody sees SDE and other supernatural events as similar to the northern lights, that ethereal glow that takes place near the north pole, a source of awe for mankind despite, or perhaps because of, their unexplained nature. My wife and I experienced the northern lights near Fairbanks, Alaska. This was our third trip to the Alaskan wilderness, but our first time experiencing these magnificent lights.

We were on a two-day dog sledding trip and were sleeping in a tent in the middle of an isolated meadow-like canyon. I say we experienced, because what happened was very different than any picture or video that we had seen of these lights. I woke to an almost childlike game of hide and seek with them. I came out of the tent and saw just a tiny glimpse of them, but still woke my wife to share what was there for us to see. Well, better than nothing, she went back into the tent, and I stayed out a while longer.

All of a sudden and seemingly out of nowhere came the most glorious light show that I had ever seen. It was crossing the sky from one hillside to the other and back again, back and forth, again and again. I called my wife out to see more of this amazing display. This time more satisfied, she went back in to warm up as the temperature was easily twenty degrees below zero. But again, I stayed out for more, and more I certainly received. The lights were circling round and round and calling me into them. I truly felt as though I was One with these heavenly lights, truly, Divinely connected with them. It was an utterly amazing and mystical moment with Cosmic Oneness.

PORTALS OF DEATH

Furthermore, Moody says that there is something about being in the presence of death, not necessarily our own, that can open a portal to a higher world, one that those who are dying can open to those who will go on living. There was a year, not long ago, when I was in the presence of several individual deaths. Some were just before, some just after, some in person, some from a distance, some seen first-hand, some related to me. But, the one that stands out clearest in my mind is the passing of a man named Lou. It is a very long story, but I will try to condense it for you.

I had been visiting with an elderly woman, Florence, the mother of a high school friend of mine. We would meet for coffee and a slice of pie each Thursday afternoon. We had been meeting monthly when something told me to start meeting weekly, and so we did.

For the better part of six months, her husband, Lou, was literally dying in the lower level of their home with nurses and hospice care. One day, I asked if I could go downstairs to have a word with her husband. I think that she thought that it would bother me to see him in his condition. I must say that I had never met Lou before, not in the high school days and not since, because when I entered their basement, Lou, who had not been talking in days, called out in a strong and clear voice, "Tom. Tom." This was more than unusual, as Lou had never met me, nor had Florence or her daughters ever spoken of me to him.

Well, let us flash-forward a couple of weeks, and I found myself deep in meditation one Monday morning. I came out with the notion of exercising, but strange to say that I went straight to the shower, dressed, got into my car and drove to Florence and Lou's house. I never knew consciously what I was doing, until I put the car in park and realized that I was in their driveway. I spent the afternoon with them in the basement. Later that day I went home for a quick shower and a cup of coffee and ended up back at their home, expecting to sit with Lou through the night. Much to my surprise, Florence went to bed shortly after I arrived, and her daughter went home for the night, so there I was, alone with Lou.

Well, I prayed and spoke softly to Lou, rubbing his forehead and letting him know that all was in Divine order, that he had lived a beautiful life and could be proud of his husbandly and fatherly accomplishments, and that it was all right to let go, and be in the place that he truly wanted to be. Lou had been breathing strong and steady all throughout the day (like a marathon runner, it seemed to me). So, when he took his last breath, it was as though his arms had risen above his head and his chest had broken the finish line tape (like the winner of a marathon race), and he was Home.

It is hard to put into words the feelings of jubilation that filled this otherwise empty room. I had expected to shed tears of sadness, but I found myself shedding tears of joy and tears of love and appreciation, for that moment was one to remember forever.

I can readily understand what Raymond Moody means when he refers to the specialness of being in the presence of such a transition, and the portal was clearly open for me, connecting the earthly realm with the Divine. The Voice is clearly why my visits changed from monthly to weekly. The Voice is clearly why I ended up in their driveway on the day of Lou's passing. The Voice gave me the words to share with Lou. Furthermore, the Voice allowed me to be in the most sacred space as Lou made his crossing into the celestial realm.

I see near-death and shared-death experiences as direct communication from the Voice. It seems as though the Divine is watching and calls a time out at momentous occasions for us to re-establish our reason for being in this particular life at this particular time. My between-life work suggests that we do have an intended purpose in each life, so, a near-death experience signals, to me, that one has drifted too far from one's original plan. To use another well-known term, Divine Intervention, seems to be occurring. For some unknown reason, the option of ending this life and starting over has been avoided, and in its place comes this Divine time out. The Voice, through the NDE, seems to inspire a new sense of purpose with new virtues and new direction. Something similar can be said of the SDEs, as they report meaningful changes in their outlooks on life and can share the inspirations that they felt as they went through their experiences.

About four years after Lou's passing, this same dear friend, Florence, fell and broke her a hip for the third time in not so many years. In past times, she was "out of it" for a day or two and came back strong. This time, she seemed distant the whole time in the hospital. Occasionally, she moved her feet when someone new or special entered the room. But most of the time, she was some-place between here and there. Each day, I wondered what was keeping her from checking out. To my pleasant surprise, each day brought some new family miracle. Two daughters, individually, experienced epiphanies that changed their lives, not deathbed promises, but true changes in perspectives on life and living that will carry them on through until their ends. Somehow, from wher-ever Florence was during this time, she was communicating to her daughters, and her daughters were listening, listening now with their hearts and not their minds. Thank God!!

I was sitting with one of Florence's grandsons and asking him what he had "going on." He said he is a musician, like many in his family. The grandson said that he plays several instruments but really loves playing the harp. He said that he was not entirely sure what he was going to do with his harp until sitting with his grandmother, Florence. It came to him that playing his harp in hospital or in hospice just might be what he is meant to do with his life. Not ten minutes later, a lady with a harp passed by the room – yes really! We asked if the grandson could play a song for Florence. Of course, she agreed, and he began to play.

Next, his mom, one of the daughters who had just experienced a life-altering epiphany, entered the room to see her son playing the harp for her mother. Wow! The Voice—stamping this woman's epiphany into permanence.

Moments like these went on for eleven days and something told me that this night would be her last. I stayed in her hospital room and spoke with her throughout the night, hoping to empty out her fears and reminding her how much she resembled her husband on the night of his transition, suggesting that we had prepared for almost five years and that all was in God's hands, offering that she let go of the body and let the angels carry her into the light.

Throughout the eleven days, I spoke and coached and tried to help her, but never really knew whether or not I was getting through to her. But in the end, Florence let me know through a remarkable gift. While with Lou, I knew that he had crossed the finish line, and I rejoiced with him as he made his way through the light, but Florence went one generous step further. The instant that her breathing stopped, she paused just before the finish line, and silently, she invited me to walk across with her, and then went into the light. What a powerful, generous gift from Florence to me, and one that I am giving to you. Incidentally, that globe of light in the Altered States chapter was Florence.

I tell you this story because it holds everything that there is to say about living, loving, preparing for transition, the place beyond, crossing the finish line, communicating from beyond with those still here, timelessness, spacelessness, relationship with loved ones and with God. Whatever she had accomplished during her eighty-nine years on this planet was dwarfed by what she accomplished in her final days. The gifts that she gave to me, to her daughters, to her grandchildren, and to you are beyond words. To you she gives the gift of knowledge and wisdom from far beyond our intellects about life and purpose and living beyond this human incarnation. Florence offers hope and support to your own aspirations and intentions for living a happy and purposeful life.

Regardless of what skeptics say about the science of these experiences, we, who have seen for ourselves, know of the spiritual benefits of going through them. The question for humanity might be, "How can we bottle these benefits for others to experience?" One of the biggest challenges of attempting to bottle the spiritual benefits of near-death and shared-death experiences is that the experiences themselves are random and unexpected. We never know, in advance, if one of these powerful experiences is about to occur.

Another big challenge is that the person comes incredibly close to death in one case, and in the other case, the person actually dies. So, if we were to attempt to gather the spiritual gems of these experiences for life-changing benefits, we would have to come close to or, in fact, die. Neither outcome is all that comforting in advance. We can probably forget about attracting volunteers to the study of these phenomena.

PROCESS TO ENTER THE PORTALS

Raymond Moody pondered this dilemma for quite some time. He was keen on finding a way for people to reap the spiritual and psychological benefits of (NDE) and (SDE). Moody went back to his ancient Greek roots and focused on the Oracles of the Dead and how they helped individuals make healing contact with departed loved ones. He discovered a very basic, three-step process for reaping the benefits of contact with deceased loved ones, and he modernized these three steps so that they could be easily replicated and repeated without having to come to near brushes with death.

The first step is to prepare the client for his or her upcoming visit with the departed loved one. The Oracles of the Dead spent something like thirty days preparing the person. It was clear to Raymond Moody that the demands that we put on ourselves these days would not allow for a thirty day wait. Instead, he condensed the preparation to several hours, not days, of concentrated talking and evoking of thoughts and memories about the deceased loved one. Speaking and listening from the heart, Raymond and others can bring forth quite a bit of stored information, some of which seems hidden from the one who plans to visit. While there is no set time limit for the preparatory conversation, it becomes pretty clear when the time has come for step two, the actual visitation.

The Oracles would sit the person in front of a large container of water, wine, olive oil, or some other liquid with reflective qualities. The container would be sitting in a very dark place, usually in an underground cave-like setting, dimly lit by torch or candles. The seekers were to gaze into the reflective substance and the departed loved one would appear, not in memories, but in real-time conversational mode. The person would converse with the departed as long as they liked or until the visitor faded back to its celestial home.

Raymond Moody suspected that most people would be fearful of dark, musty, cave-like settings, so, he created his version of the *psychomanteum,* a small room, walls and ceiling painted black, a mirror on the wall, a comfortable chair and a candle behind the chair to allow just enough light to observe what comes into the mirror, but still leaving the dimly lit feeling of wonder and excitement. The person sits in the chair and waits patiently for his or her visit to begin, stays as long as is wanted and leaves the room when the visit is finished. All the while, Raymond is sitting outside the room, waiting for step three, a thorough vetting of what transpired in the mirror and the first impressions of what might be the intended purpose of the visitation.

In olden times, the Oracles would interpret what the visitation was about for the person. In Moody's view, it is much more important that the client do the interpreting, but is glad to help or support in any way that he can. Step three is the immediate downloading of images and impressions and messages received by the living from the deceased. Again, no time limits here, this can take as long as one wishes, knowing that more will come to mind that night and over the next few days or even weeks. Placing the immediate impressions out on the table is important to the process.

That is Raymond's theory and practice, one that he has been observing for several decades with hundreds of people coming through his *psychomanteum*. Do we just take his word for it, or do we try it for ourselves? Well, if you say that I would not be writing this if I had not gone there myself, you would be correct. The very nature of my inquiry in our discoveries is about direct and personal access into the mystical realm, to hear what the Voice has to offer to us. Therefore, I contacted Dr. Moody and asked if I could come sit with him and in his mirror gazing room to experience for myself this afterlife visitation method that the ancient Greeks and others have used so powerfully. I say others because indigenous peoples all over the world have spoken of such powerful visitation rituals.

Native American Indians used water at the edges of ponds, lakes, creeks and rivers. Other reflective surfaces have been used as well. Breaking news: wishing wells and fountains were not just a means for collecting and displaying coins. They were originally used to serve as surfaces for the evoked visitation. Later on, they became known for making wishes. More breaking news: Aladdin's lamp was not about forcing the genie out of the bottle. Rather, the rubbing of the metal lamp was to clear the way for the deceased to appear on the outside of the lamp. Sorry to crush any childhood memories here.

Soon, I went to Alabama and spent an incredible day with Raymond Moody and his lovely wife, Cheryl. My purpose was to experience, first hand, this mysteriously communicative modality and bring back to you an inspiring story. My intention for this journey was much more than idle curiosity or entertainment. My intention was to visit this ancient method and to see and hear for myself the Voice coming through this sacred experience. I did come back with a powerfully moving story. I hope you feel moved after hearing it.

To the animal lovers, and I definitely include myself in this category, I will begin by saying that on my drive from the hotel to the Moody house, I crossed paths with a family of white cattle grazing peacefully in a nearby meadow. White animals are considered powerful totems, and I genuinely felt their participation in my journey as I passed by them.

I spent the full day, Tuesday, at the Moody home. During our preliminary conversations, Raymond described the three most likely outcomes of spending time in his mirror gazing room, at least as reported by hundreds of experiencers over the past twenty-some years. The three outcomes might be 1) my intended visitor would speak to me from the mirror, 2) I would leave my body and enter the mirror for conversation, or 3) the visitor would leave the mirror and join me, three-dimensionally, in the room for conversation. There was a fourth outcome, which I will mention a bit later in this story, for reasons that will then make sense.

Before Raymond and I went too deep into conversation, his wife, Cheryl, called us over to what she called a light lunch. Actually, it was a glorious spread of fresh fruits, cheeses and smoked salmon (a favorite of mine). The lunch was truly a time of bonding and connection. During our lunch conversation, I mentioned a story of a most unusual experience with a woman named Bernadette and her son-in-law. This begins the story within the story.

STORY WITHIN THE STORY

My elderly friend, Florence, had been living in a seniors' assisted living home for the past three years. I was visiting Florence and a handful of ladies each Thursday. Bernadette had joined us in brief conversation a number of times and then began joining us for lunch on the first Thursday of each month. Quite soon after meeting Bernadette, she asked me to pray for her son-in-law, as he was that day, going through a five-hour surgery on a leaking brain tumor. I said that I would pray and asked where this surgery was taking place. She told me, and I said that I would visit him the next day, as I would be, coincidentally, driving my mom and step-dad to that very hospital for a doctor's visit. Bernadette seemed relieved, and I wondered to myself how exactly I would get to the room of someone who had just the day before undergone such serious surgery.

Well, the next day came and I found myself in the elevator with a room tag on my shirt collar, heading to the son-in-law's room. As the elevator doors opened I noticed a strong feeling flow through me with the words, "This is important." I walked through the very intensive care unit as if I knew where I was going and was expected to be there. Not a single nurse or doctor questioned my presence. I entered his room, introduced myself and my connection to Bernadette, and instantly found the two of us in a deeply spiritually conversation, the thrust of which had to do with his holding the utmost faith in the Lord as he was facing his physical challenges. Incidentally, I should mention that his wife, Bernadette's daughter, was in late-stage leukemia at this same time. Nurses came and took blood. Other bodily fluids were drawn as well as we continued our conversation. Finally, a team of doctors entered the room, and I took my cue to shake his hand and say, "Keep going, you are doing exactly what you need to be doing," and I left the hospital room.

I saw Bernadette the next week and she reported that her son-in-law had very much enjoyed our visit and that he knew me. She challenged him as she had just recently met me herself. But he was certain in his understanding that he knew *me*. A month later, Bernadette reported to me that both her son-in-law and her daughter were in steady remission.

I related this story to Raymond and Cheryl and heard myself say, "I don't know why I am telling you this." After finishing lunch, Raymond and I headed to his third floor mirror gazing room. We spoke together for quite a while before I entered the mirror room, and Raymond sat outside the door to the room. I said to myself that I was here on behalf of whoever needed this the most. Not long into the session, my cell phone vibrated, and I left it alone until I returned to my hotel, so I had no idea at the time who called or what he or she wanted of me.

For the better part of the next three hours, I sat with high spiritual voltage running through my body and watching a most amazing parade of faces and eyes coming towards me. There were adults and children and animals and in particular, a golden eagle that flew to me through the center of the mirror. I had seen this eagle in other spiritual moments previously. By the end of the session, I felt spiritually enlivened, overpowered and spent.

Raymond most kindly re-assured me that not having experienced any of the three possibilities was not a failure. That I saw what I saw was proof enough that I would see what I needed to see when the time is right. I said that I would practice the method at home, and I still do.

I arrived back at my hotel and saw that it was Bernadette who had called. She left a message of apology for having missed the last few luncheons and wanted desperately to rejoin us. I called her back and gladly extended the invitation to join us on Thursday, as it was the first Thursday of this new month. She was thrilled and did join us for lunch. I shared some of the details of my Tuesday experience with Florence and Bernadette and said that I was certain that it was real by the spiritual voltage that had run through my body as I sat in front of the mirror.

Bernadette said that those things do not happen to her, just to people like me. I assured her that she was wrong and asked if she had ever felt such a loving flow inside her that she cried. I said that crying was the body's reaction to the overpowering flow of love. Well, she started crying just then. She shared that just Tuesday she had been sitting in her living room, and her deceased husband came to her, in three-dimensional form, to tell her how much he loved her, and that she held him in her arms as they spoke, cried while he was there and cried after he left. She spoke so matter-of-factly, and the three of us found ourselves sharing tears.

Bernadette thought that she was telling us a story about crying, while I knew that she was telling us a story about visitation. I told Bernadette that her husband had truly come to visit her, that Tuesday's moment was not a dream. As a matter of fact, it was the fourth possibility that Raymond and I had discussed, that a totally different person than the one sitting in front of the mirror might have the experience. He calls it "apparition by proxy." Truly I say, "Bernadette had this experience!"

BENEFITS OF A NEAR-DEATH EXPERIENCE

Raymond Moody's intention of creating the benefits of a near-death experience without needing to be near death had come forth magnificently! Bernadette was re-booted and re-inspired in the way similar to how Ebenezer Scrooge was the morning after his time with the ghosts of Christmas past, present and future. She spoke of having not been as good a person as she wished that she had been to this point and how she was going to be a much better person going forward. She is inspired to live a more loving, accepting and giving life now. That is precisely what happens through a near-death experience. Wow!!

Does the story end here? Not exactly! Over the next few days I was approached, unsolicited, by several dear friends who had no idea that I was involved with mirror gazing or visitations from the deceased. They came to me because they did not know who else might understand what they had to say. Their stories were nearly identical to Bernadette's.

One friend called to say that her grandfather had come to visit. As a child she had idolized her grandfather, and his recent visit was vivid, lucid, three-dimensional and incredibly moving

Another friend told me of a visit from two grandparents at once. She was sitting on her couch one afternoon and all of a sudden, there they were, standing right in front of her. I asked if she had been sleeping, and she responded that she was sure that she had not been. They came with a message of loving support and encouragement. They wanted her to know that they were well aware of her struggles, and that she could call on them whenever she felt the need.

Another friend is facing physical challenges brought about by Alzheimer's. He had been an athlete all his life, so these challenges have been hard for him to handle. The last six months have been particularly tough for him. On a visit the week after my mirror gazing with Raymond, he reported to me that his father had come to visit him on that same Tuesday afternoon. Had his wife been out of the house at the time, who knows how his news would have been received? But she was there to witness, not the dad, but her husband's standing and holding and speaking with his dad. She saw his eyes light up with love and appreciation for his father's timely visit of support and love for his son. Again, the visit was very much three dimensional in nature.

Hearing these timely and unsolicited stories of three-dimensional visits from deceased loved ones made me stop and wonder what and why this was going on in my life and in my awareness. After much prayerful contemplation, it became quite clear that this information was for me to know in so far as it leads to your knowing of this powerfully spiritual phenomenon. My stated intention was to be in front of Raymond Moody's mirror for whoever needed it the most. And clearly, those that needed the visits received them in concert with the Voice of Divinity, shared with them through me. What an honor it is to share these Divine moments with you.

OTHER PROCESS MODALITIES

A few months after these visitations, Dr. Raymond Moody and Dr. Calen Rayne teamed up to offer a course on mirror gazing and supporting energy work. I call Calen Rayne the energy doctor, as, in my view, he is more aware of transformational and ritual energies and vibrations than anyone I have come across. He has studied and mastered many of the most ancient forms of energy healing, and applies his knowledge to labyrinth building, reiki healing, energy space clearing, as well as intuitive and pastoral counseling.

To prepare for this course we read what little had been written about the history of crystal gazing and scrying. These are two modalities that come closest to mirror gazing and have been used for centuries as means of looking into remote or future events. The materials came alive as an historical introduction to modalities somewhat related to mirror gazing, but the real coming to life occurred at Calen Rayne's home in Asheville, North Carolina where the course was held. The upstairs was our artist loft where we learned energy-painting techniques. The downstairs was our temple, loaded with altars and artifacts from around the world and home to Calen's recently built *psychomanteum*.

Beginning each day with a mild group meditation opened us up to the flow that came our way from early morning on through to late night discussions. The topics of the mornings were centered around mirror gazing, the afternoons were centered around creating personal altars and paintings, and the evenings neatly combined the two.

Having been acquainted with mirror gazing by Raymond and altar building and painting by Calen, we were allowed to partner up and experience Rayne's mirror gazing room. I have to say that I was and am still deeply moved by the partnership experience that I personally encountered.

Having already experienced Raymond's mirror room, my primary interest was in helping my study partner through her visitation. She and I sat down on the porch and dove deeply into the memories of her departed mother. We talked freely and frankly and touched many sensitive and hidden thoughts from their years as mother and daughter. We did not have all day, as was my case at Raymond's home, but we "wrung out" the feelings fairly well. Without divulging personal particulars, I think that I can say that two key spiritual connections were with the Black Madonna and St. Therese of Liseux, the "little flower." My partner felt as prepared as could be and entered the mirror gazing room hoping to visit with her mother and perhaps resolve any missing parts of their relationship.

While she was in the mirror room, I felt compelled to make her an altar and paint her a picture that seemed to reflect the connection that mother and daughter had to one another. What came off of my brush was a rather mysterious Madonna coming out of the water.

My partner came out of the room after about an hour and reported no visitation. We agreed that all was not lost, as we were both first timers in the roles that we were playing. However, we did continue our conversation for a few more hours and ended the day in very good spirits.

My partner went to her hotel, and I stayed at the Rayne's (where I was fortunate to be staying for the week). Calen, his wife and I were watching the eleven o'clock news, when suddenly I felt a strong urge to head to the loft to paint a different painting for my study partner. The overwhelming sense was that the Madonna should have roses, so I grabbed the paint and brushes and produced a new, better reflection of St. Therese, with a garland of red roses round her neck and flowing to the floor. The next morning, my partner reported to the group that her mother had visited her in a dream with beautiful words. Well, there were no dry eyes in the room as we all shared in her glory.

The connection had been made, like my earlier visit with Raymond, after sitting in front of the mirror but not necessarily through the mirror. Was the intention greater than the phenomenon? I am beginning to wonder.

There is a bit more to the story, which needs sharing. I happen to live near the national shrine to St. Therese of Liseux. I go there from time to time. I went there to take some pictures to turn into a memento of the experience for my study partner. I have done this before, so I only went to see if there was anything new to add to my photo collection of the shrine. Well, looking around I came across a new glass casing with a few new items from France. I took a close look and to my astonishment there was a note about the love St. Therese had for painting and a handful of her old paintbrushes. Awestruck, I wondered who it was that sent me back to redo the painting. Originally, I thought of my study partner's mother. But with those paintbrushes staring me in the face, I could not help but wonder if it was not St. Therese, herself.

This journey that we have been on, through the energies of mirror gazing and other related experiences, was meant to open up our minds to the incredible possibilities that are available to us in this lifetime. Like the experiences of (NDE) and (SDE), we have been shown that life exists far beyond our limited imaginations. When we listen to the Voice of Divinity, we are guided to places and feelings that so often become overlooked or lost in the meaningless details of life. These opportunities are not just offered to avatars, prophets and saints. They are offered to each and every one of us. It is up to us to desire the connection with our Creator that opens us up to Truth and Ultimate Freedom. We have to reach out for the Hand of God, like George Harrison, not just on our deathbeds, but all throughout our lifetimes. The celestial visitors tell us that all is love, and that we are whole and complete and that heaven is within us. We can stop searching outside and listen inside for Truth, Love, Power and Happiness. That is what they tell me. I hope that you are beginning to feel the same.

THE BUDDHA'S SEEKING

The Buddha is said to have spent an incredible amount of time in deep meditation. Much of the time his body was weakened by prolonged fasting. I can imagine what a medical professional might have thought upon seeing him in his far-off state. Would they have

considered him near-dead? It is hard to know. However, some of the following words from
The Dhammapada strike the NDE cord with me.

From the verse called, "Flowers," comes,

As a garland-maker chooses the right flowers, choose the well-taught path of
dharma and go beyond the realms of death and of the gods. As a garland-maker
chooses the right flowers, those who choose the well-taught path of dharma will
go beyond the realms of death and of the gods. (Easwaran, 1985, p. 117)

The garland of flowers that I placed on the dark woman in the painting for my study
partner seemed to open the door to the visitation between my study partner and her mother.
Clearly to me, the realm that they were visiting was the realm beyond death. That St.
Therese touched me both at the time, and as I was creating the video, definitely brought me
closer to communication from the realm beyond death.

From the verse called, "Thousands," it is stated, "One day's glimpse of the deathless
state is better than a hundred years of life without it. One day's glimpse of dharma is bet-
ter than a hundred years of life without it" (Easwaran, 1985, p. 136). These could be the
words from almost any near-death experiencer and sound virtually identical to what Eben
Alexander uttered about his time in the beyond. The character playing Ebeneezer Scrooge
in Dickens' Christmas Carol definitely displayed this type of joyful energy.

From the verse called, "The Path," it is written,

Death comes and carries off a man absorbed in his family and possessions as the
monsoon flood sweeps away a sleeping village. Neither children nor parents can
rescue one whom death has seized. Remember this, and follow without delay the
path that leads to nirvana. (Easwaran, 1985, p. 207)

Yes, but we are being told and actually seeing that the child and parent can reconnect in this lifetime. So, is rescue really necessary when we can converse with our deceased loved ones between paradigms? The crossing over between the celestial realm and the earthly realm seems to be a real and worthwhile activity, particularly when it brings healing to the earthly soul.

From the verse called, "Varied Verses," the Buddha states, "If one who enjoys a lesser happiness beholds a greater one, let him leave aside the lesser to gain the greater" (Easwaran, 1985, p. 211). This is perhaps the greatest challenge of the near-death experience: That the celestial realm is so loving and beautiful, makes returning to the earthly life such a difficult decision. Many NDEs report not really wanting to return. That is what makes their return so magnificent. They almost invariably return because of the love that they have for someone still earthbound. They actually choose to leave the blissful state for the love of their parent, child, sibling or other. It is absolutely amazing!

From the verse called, "Varied Verses," Buddha states, "It is hard to leave the world and hard to live in it, painful to live with the worldly and painful to be a wanderer. Reach the goal; you will wander and suffer no more" (Easwaran, 1985, p. 213). I am not so sure that I agree with the Buddha on this one. The message that comes to the living from those who have passed on is almost always that they are in a good place and that the loved one need not worry about them. Furthermore, that they are still very much aware of the loved one's life, and all the pains and pleasures that they are experiencing here on earth. The message seems to be more that happiness is still very possible here on earth. The Voice seems to be offering inspiration to keep on going in this lifetime.

CHAPTER 6
Pilgrimages to Sacred Places
▲▲▲

LET ME SHARE A FEW general comments about pilgrimage before we journey into three powerful personal pilgrimages that displayed the Voice in rarified form. First, I have noticed that pilgrimages are truly inspired events, journeys that we feel deeply called to undertake. Sometimes, they have felt like places that I have been before and felt the need to return. Other times, they felt like some place that I had always longed to visit, without understanding the reasons why. Still, other times, there was the sense of being mystically invited to make the journey to the particular location, only to find out *why* once I had arrived there.

Second, the journey to the pilgrimage site has usually been onerous, sometimes beyond challenging. In this day and age, and from my vantage point, traveling to the sacred site was usually complicated with many overlapping arrangements, connections, time zones, languages, with the use of planes, trains, buses and automobiles to make it to the intended destination. With these challenges, I could either tie up in knots of frustration or simply go with the flow.

Third, the pilgrimage, itself, is not all about floating in a sea of incense, flowers and heavenly music. The pilgrimages that I have taken have been wildly energetic in both positive and negative ways. Naturally, the end result is absolutely positive and beyond my expectations. However, clear-cut challenges have presented themselves in the course of my time spent on pilgrimage.

First Pilgrimage

The first pilgrimage that I would like to describe was my journey to the historic Chartres Cathedral located in Chartres, France, about 80 miles southwest of Paris. The planning for and journeying to Chartres was indeed complicated and challenging. Located in a foreign country, but not in a major city, there were additional layers of complexity. Airline tickets needed to be purchased; a railroad pass from Paris to Chartres had to be found and purchased, relying much on faith as the internet was barely helpful in this regard; a bus or taxi needed to be found that would take me from the airport to the train station. Inside the train station, where to pick up the tickets and where to board which train on which platform was a tremendous challenge as I was mightily inhibited by the foreign language; and even when to exit the train required some faith and collaboration with other riders, again language challenged. All of these connections had to be properly timed, as to miss a connection would have been disastrous. Needless to say, many of the same complications re-appeared for the return trip home. Fortunately, the walk from the Chartres train station was uneventful; but, the location of the hotel that I had selected, again through the internet, was a fair distance from the cathedral. So, I hope that I have established that the journey to this pilgrimage site was eventful.

The "why" I felt called to Chartres and the "how I was invited" concepts might spring out of the following words. A handful of years prior to this pilgrimage I was studying under a very special spiritual teacher. This powerful teacher often spoke of the inspirational beauty of Chartres Cathedral. He spoke of it as if it were the most glorious place on earth to sit and just soak in all the love that is here for us. I was drawn to the internet to investigate from a distance and came across a really well-done DVD that described this magnificent cathedral through pictures and through conversations with a cathedral guide. (Incidentally, once in the cathedral, I noticed this same guide was leading a group through the cathedral as he had done on the DVD. What a *déjà vu* moment that produced for me.) Through the heart-felt descriptions from my teacher and this DVD, I had a pretty good sense that I would make my way to this Chartres Cathedral someday, and, of course, I did.

The second concept that I want to share has to do with a birthday present that my mother had given me a few years before heading to Chartres. I was used to receiving unusual gifts from my mother, so when she gave me a framed, 18th century map of France, I was not overly shocked. Not knowing why she had given it to me; yet, being the good son that I am, I hung this framed French map in my study.

It was not until a year or so after returning from this pilgrimage that the Voice spoke to me during a prayerful meditation. The Voice said, "Look at that map." I took the map down to get a good look at it for the first time and discovered something rather startling. This map of France had lines from all directions centering on a very particular spot. Can you begin to imagine what that very particular spot was? Correct, all the lines came together at Chartres. Additionally, the map had a few simple sketch drawings of the town and cathedral of Chartres, the coat of arms of Chartres, and sketches of three noted Chartres characters. A bit dazed, I called my mother to ask if she knew why she had given me this particular gift, and she did not really know. I shared what was on this map and we both let out a mystical sigh of amazement.

Lastly, I need to say that the moment that I stepped off of the train and into the little town of Chartres, I knew that I was in a very mysterious, energetic and mystical place. As I walked to my hotel, I felt an energy swirling around and through me. When I arrived at my hotel, my room was not yet ready (big surprise), so I walked some more through the little village and absorbed more of this beautiful energy. The moment that I stepped into the cathedral, I knew exactly why I had come.

So here I was in Chartres, France, attending a weeklong investigation into the Mysteries of Sacred Geometry, and at the center was the cathedral itself. Roughly a hundred of us had gathered from all over the world. There were teachers, students, math lovers and spiritualists alike. But, here came one of the challenges that I previously mentioned. Right "off the bat" and all throughout the week I heard pronouncements from one of the lead teachers that troubled me. He said, "Through the eyes (from a quote) of Heraclitus, nature is wont to hide herself, and what seems so clear is clear because nature is hiding the essence. What we think we know actually leads us away from the Truth, because nature hides knowledge. Furthermore, there is a Divine veil that we are not only not to peek behind, but that we will be severely punished if we do, as in the cases of Acteon, who was turned into a stag and was devoured by his own hunting party, and Semele, mother of Dionysus, who went up in flames after being tricked by a jealous wife into seeing the real Jupiter" (Garrison, lecture, 7/4/11).

As a youngster, I absolutely loved Greek, Roman and Egyptian mythology, and I have no quarrel with the accuracy of these stories told to us at Chartres. My problem is that I do not believe that Divinity wants to hide from us, or worse yet, to punish us for seeing what is *real* about Divinity. Everything that I seem to know about our conversation with the Voice, the whole reason for this discovery writing, suggests exactly the opposite of what I was hearing from this teacher. Perhaps the Voice is asking us to take a second look at the perceptions of what has been said, not only here in Chartres, but often through recorded history. Is the Voice asking us to think again about our relationship with Divinity and reconsider the conversation that we are having with It? It sure seems so to me.

I would be more inclined to consider the Heraclitus quote, "The lord who is the Oracles at Delphi neither utters nor hides his meaning, but shows it by a sign" (Goodreads.com, 2011). From where I live on the spiritual path, I thank the Lord daily for each and every opportunity to feel the love and share the love with His children. I have to believe (mostly from my own experience) that the further along the path that we travel, the more frequent the *signs* appear for us to see and enjoy and share with others. Heraclitus also said, "Thinking is a sacred disease, and sight is deception" (Goodreads.com, 2011). But, geometer Richard Henry in Chartres offered, "It helps to look at the world with soft eyes as the essence is not obvious with hard eyes" (lecture, 7/5/11). I do not think that it is so much Divinity hiding; but rather, how we look at things, with soft, contemplative, compassionate eyes or with hard, analytical, judgmental eyes, that determines what we actually see.

One last Heraclitus quote says, "Eyes and ears are poor witnesses to people if they have uncultured souls" (Goodreads.com, 2011). With fear in our hearts we experience a whole different world than when we have love in our hearts. Only by truly surrendering ourselves to Divinity do these mystical opportunities present themselves. It is almost as if, when we are ready to see, we are able to see the Divine majesty that is there for us. We do not need Divinity to hide Its secrets from us. We can do a pretty good job of missing all the love that is right in front of our noses. Ancient Upanishads believed God would hide in a man or woman, as humans would never think to look there to find God (Easwaran, 1985). So, here we have some extreme tension between what fearful instincts are saying about hiding, and what loving intuitions are saying about seeking. No doubt, the Voice has something more to say about this.

Moving beyond philosophy and straight to practicality, I would say that this whole week in sacred space was overloaded with signs from the Voice of what Sacred Geometry is all about. As a spiritual teacher as well as a teacher of mathematics, I was overjoyed to be in this sacred space. So many spiritually talented and loving people (teachers and students) made their ways to Chartres at this particular time, to experience Sacred Geometry in the most Divine way. This program was filled with many incredible ways to experience Sacred Geometry: music, art, song, astrology, mythology, hands-on geometry, crop circle discovery, cosmetology, freemasonry, Buddhism, dreams, and on and on, not to mention the most incredibly Divine presence of the Chartres Cathedral itself.

There was such a strong sense of Oneness throughout this group as we worked together to find our way through Sacred Geometry in all its magnificence. I like to connect dots, and there are just so many dots here that connect to the point that Divinity wants us to see Itself in all Its radiant glory. This week's experiences were definitely there for us to see. Absolutely nothing was hidden from us, as far as I could tell. Thank you, Voice.

There were many mystically moving moments of Sacred Geometry brought through Chartres Cathedral throughout the week. An especially moving moment, most likely my reason for being at Chartres, came through the group of us singing the "Alleluia Chorus" around the sacred labyrinth in Chartres Cathedral. This moment, for me, came as a result of stretching far beyond my original comfort zone and seeing myself being pulled into a much larger and loving zone. Some in our group gathered each afternoon to practice singing this and a few other challenging pieces. Many of these people were talented singers. My wife is the classically trained voice in our family. I certainly am not. The practices stretched far beyond my singing skills. But, they paid off handsomely as the moment arrived in a glorious manner.

Our whole group walked the labyrinth together, building spiritual energies, and with a crescendo coming as we gathered in a circle surrounding the candle-lit labyrinth and began singing the "Alleluia" in three-part harmony. Platonists were said to believe that supernatural moments came from a simultaneous interweaving, epitomized through the sounding of the octave, which produces the essential spirits of vocal harmony. Well, holding hands in a circle around the candle-lit labyrinth that was teaming with spiritual stimulation, we began singing round and round, Pachelbel's "Canon."

It seemed to me that each time around, my voice became clearer and stronger. Next, I noticed that the group's voice was growing clearer and stronger as well. I found my whole body shaking and tears running down my face as the Divine beauty of our Voice came through this most beautiful song. Wow, what a feeling! The next day I could not help but share with the group my perception of how our Voice had come through us so clearly the night before. That we all had much to share with humanity, and that this was a clear reminder, from the Voice, that we should be doing so. I cannot tell you how many students came up to me over the next few days to say thank you for my sharing. They felt honored, empowered and supported by the message that I had shared with them. However, the reminder to be the Voice was certainly not coming from me, but rather, coming through me. I was humbly grateful to have a Voice to do so when the opportunity presented itself.

Second Pilgrimage

The second journey of pilgrimage involves Chartres, in a way, but precedes the first pilgrimage chronologically by about a year. This pilgrimage was to Sedona, Arizona, to spend time with the powerful spiritual teacher who spoke so highly of Chartres Cathedral. Truth be told, I did not spend any time with the teacher, in a physical presence, but lived right next door to him for seven weeks.

Here is how this pilgrimage came about. One day I felt a powerful swirling energy flow through me, and its Voice said to come to Sedona. This seemed a bit odd as my wife and I had been to Sedona, to see the teacher, several times in the prior few years. It was not as though I needed another trip to Sedona.

The very next day, a dear friend, who owned the house right next door to the teacher, called me to say that the day before (same day as my swirling energy) he had a strong message from consciousness (his words) that told him to offer me his home for as short or as long as I wanted it. He and his wife had moved away but had not yet sold this empty house. (This is the same couple that I mentioned in the Washington state horse story.) When I say right next door to the teacher, I mean three small houses behind a security gate with no one else around for ten acres, except deer and javelinas. This property sat along Oak Creek with Cathedral Rock just across from it. The rhythmic sound of the creek was always in my ear, and the majestic rock was always in my eyesight.

Given what the Voice was offering through my friend, my wife and I quickly re-arranged our lives to take advantage of the gift that was being given. My wife and I decided that she would drive with me to Sedona and spend the weekend, then fly back home and return two months later to help me drive back home. We were bringing our two Alaskan huskies; so, I traded in my sedan for a dog-friendly car. We packed up my stuff, our dogs and hit the road to Sedona.

Harley, our original Alaskan husky, had been suffering from liver cancer for all of the prior year. He was not really meant to last the Sedona visit, as he passed the night after our arrival. We have a picture of him happily gazing out the car window on his last road trip. I felt honored that he travelled with me to my pilgrimage site. Rosie, our second Alaskan husky, was very new to us, so the pilgrimage was really like throwing her into the deep end of the spiritual swimming pool. She and I were really able to establish a powerful spiritual relationship together in Sedona.

While on pilgrimage, Rosie and I walked the ten acres each day, enjoying the many paths and the creek. We lived a very simple life while in Sedona. There was no television, no internet, and bad cell phone reception. We had to drive up to the local library to get in touch with my wife back home. After our morning walk and breakfast, Rosie slept as I read, prayed and meditated. We walked again in the afternoon after sometimes running errands. We ate a simple dinner, watched a spiritual DVD, and early to bed we went. The only electronic treat that I allowed myself was a nightly movie on loan from the library.

We kept as our themes investigating religions, people and historical events. Early on we tried skyping the study group from the library parking lot, where reception was better than at the house. But even that seemed to become a bit too linear for us, so we retreated back to minimal electronics.

While we had established simple routines, time was really not present on this pilgrimage. Reading, praying and meditating all blended together in powerful ways for me. Rosie received a real taste of the powerful energies that come along with this lifestyle. After a particularly deep meditation, I noticed Rosie crawling towards me on her front paws, checking to see if I was the same guy who was taking care of her. I distinctly remember on Thanksgiving Day, I had awakened to a very powerful meditation. Rosie, who had become used to sleeping on the bed, laid there for many hours, breathing but not moving. I was more than a bit distraught, as I thought that I was losing her for some unknown reason. Turns out, she was probably just stunned by the powerful energies of the meditation, or was in a sacred place of her own.

As I mentioned earlier, the teacher and I never actually met in person, even though we were living just fifty feet apart from one another. I sent over to him a copy of the Chartres DVD as a kind of invitation to be together. His wife was being very protective of his health and never responded to my offer to meet with him, even though she knew me as a true and loyal student of her husband.

Everyone back home assumed that we had spent time together. But, to me, it never truly mattered. The whole seven-week pilgrimage was about going deep inside myself without distractions from people or electronics, and finding a profound sense of direction for the coming years. This pilgrimage did all that I could ever have imagined in spite of not spending time with the teacher. So, when it was time to leave, I returned home with huge gratitude and humility for all that I was shown and given during these seven weeks.

A very curious thing happened about two months after returning home. A dear friend of mine, also a student of this teacher, wrote to me in the middle of the night. She said that she had just awoken from a very lucid and vivid dream about the teacher and me that she wanted to share before falling back to sleep. She said that the teacher was thanking me for the wonderful time that we had shared together during my seven weeks in Sedona. He mentioned something that only I would know. Then he offered some advice for my coming years. She said that he had his arm around my shoulder as we spoke as if comforting me in some way.

What my friend did not know was that I had seen this teacher unbeknownst to me at the time, in a dream some years prior, and when I came across his voice on a CD, I nearly crashed my car. I was on my way to yoga class, heard his voice, knew that something very surreal was coming to me, called my wife to see if she had ever heard of him, and found us in his audience less than a month later.

The day before this first trip to Sedona, I visited my doctor for a routine check-up. I had been taking blood pressure pills with hopes of reducing my blood pressure from around 140/110. On that particular visit, the nurse announced my blood pressure to be 100/60. I said that that could not be. She took it again, and sure enough—100/60.

You can judge for yourself what all this means to you. To me, Voiceprints are all over this seven-week pilgrimage to Sedona, spending time with this teacher and taking myself to places within that I had never dreamed possible. I believe that the call from the friend to offer his home in Sedona was through the Voice. The insights and delights of my time in Sedona were through the Voice. The mind-to-mind conversations between the teacher and me were through the Voice. And finally, the thank you message from the teacher that came through my friend's vivid dream was again through the Voice. Oh, and the blood pressure reading was a sign from the Voice that we were heading in the right direction by spending time with this particular teacher.

By the way, on our drive back home in my very new car, we ran over something that caused a flat in one of the new tires. This particular car had one of those mini-tires as a spare, which are only to be driven at slow speeds. Needless to say, that caused a bit of a problem on the open highway that stretches across the state of Nebraska. Cars and trucks were generally driving at speeds more like 75 to 80 mph. As night came on and darkness set in, a big yellow truck decided to ride just behind us for the better part of two hours, as we made our way to Omaha. If you were to say that the Voice sent us a guardian angel to protect us during these last two hours, I would not quarrel with you one bit.

THIRD PILGRIMAGE

The last pilgrimage that I want to share with you was my journey to Teotihuacan, the ancient Toltec pyramids located just north of Mexico City, Mexico. Perhaps the best way to start my description of this journey is to share a remark that occurred just as it was coming to completion. In a reflective conversation I was asked, after living through the powerful experiences of Teotihuacan, "How will you transition back into the daily routines of ordinary life?" There seemed to be a built-in assumption inside this question that suggested that after leaving Teotihuacan, I might need help getting through the many people that I would have to face as I re-enter my daily life. I said that I was not worried, that I always find that I just float back into the scenes of life without seeing or feeling stress or concern or strife on my way back from these sacred trips. It is as though I am riding the magic carpet back to my friends and family, and everyone that I pass along the way feel like friends and family to me.

Quite frankly, I said, it is the way to Teotihuacan that causes any of the stress and suffering that I feel. It is the way to the pilgrimage, for me, that I have to transition, adjust, and notice the discomfort. I think that this is a part of what pilgrimage is all about. From the moment that we leave the comforts of our homes, we feel the weight of the journey to the place that we honor so deeply. That is exactly how I feel about my journey to Teotihuacan. A bit later that same evening, as we sat in our comfortable meeting room, physically exhausted, yet spiritually invigorated from the week, again reflecting on the experiences of the week, with thunder and lightning powerfully accentuating our thoughts, my little friend Lillie, a white-haired, sparkling blue-eyed, seventy-something woman of Celtic and Lakota lineages, asked me what I would be bringing home from Teotihuacan. Without a moment's hesitation, I uttered, "I am bringing back just exactly what I came here for – the message from the Voice of Divinity as spoken through the energy flow of Teotihuacan." And now it is time for me to share with you this message from the Voice as spoken through the energy flow of Teotihuacan, because, my friends, it is you for whom this message is intended.

Let me start by saying that Teotihuacan is a powerful spot with a powerful energy flow. We have just witnessed the powerful sacred geometry of Chartres Cathedral and the powerful vortexes of Sedona, Arizona. We have seen the powerful northern lights of Fairbanks, Alaska, and so many more. So, we have a sense of what power can come through these pilgrimages, and I can safely say that Teotihuacan has its place as a powerful pilgrimage site.

Standing atop the Pyramid of the Sun, with arms outstretched, connecting the inner base of the pyramid with the heart of the Sun, brought an energy flow that was impossible to miss. Walking the Avenue of Death towards the Pyramid of the Moon, I felt the pull through the energetic umbilical cord that connected my body to that of the pyramid, step by step, as if She was reeling me into Her sacred womb. Feeling the whirling energies as I devotedly walked the labyrinth, with doves looking on, as I started each day, I felt my Oneness with the Teotihuacan energies. All of these spiritually magnificent moments are deeply moving and memorable, but none of them are the message of the Voice of Divinity as spoken through the energy flow of Teotihuacan. The message did come to and through me and here I will send it to you.

At the start of a particular day, we were told that we would be going to four very important plazas to enact four very special rituals that would bury four very important bodies that we hold onto so dearly. You might say that these four bodies were the very essence of everything that we know about ourselves. So, burying them would definitely make an impression on our psyches and our ways of seeing ourselves in the world. At the same time, we were told that in the evening, a particular woman would be leading a grief circle for us. Turns out that this woman had tragically lost her husband four years prior and would be sharing with us how she was able to work through the grief of her traumatic loss.

Well, let us flash forward a couple of hours and find ourselves in the first of four plazas, and we are being asked to bury our bodies. I say this figuratively, so you do not get the sense that we actually dug body-sized holes in the ground. We were asked to bury something and have a virtual cemetery scene, where we hear from loved ones how they feel about us in our passing time. It would be like invisibly attending your own wake or funeral ceremonies. That was pretty powerful. In the next plaza we buried our emotional bodies. Time to stop crying. In the third plaza we buried our mental bodies. Think about that one for a moment. And, in the fourth and final plaza we buried our spiritual, energy bodies. For many, this might have been the hardest body to bury, for it holds the essence of who or what we believe that we are when not in our physical, emotional and mental bodies. Any single one of these burials would have been difficult for most people. The combination of these four burials left us spent in one sense and more alive than ever in another sense. Still, we were done for the day and headed back to our quarters for food and then the grief circle.

The grief circle was much bigger than originally planned. It turned out that another woman had tragically lost her husband as well. So, the two survivors led us through the steps that they had taken to handle the losses that they faced. We appreciated their sharing of deeply moving moments in their personal lives. The next morning we went back to the Avenue of the Dead and prepared to march to the Pyramid of the Moon. Along the way, we carried our body-doubles, with intentions of offering them up to the eagle that carries them away, again releasing what we continued to hold onto. At the same time, we were asked to allow the pyramid to pull us along, as if by our umbilical cords. As I carried and was pulled along, my back felt the strain and legs began to sweat. My core muscles were registering. I was very much in tune with this particular sacred ritual. By the time that I arrived at our meeting place, my energy was bursting inside of me. We were asked to partner up and take turns comforting each other. We did a lot of partnering during the week, but this turned out to be the moment that we have been waiting for all along. I reflected back to my morning labyrinth walk, when I asked the Divine Feminine for the clearest of messages of the week, and this surely was about to be that message.

The speaker of the grief circle asked me to be her partner, and I agreed. This same woman and I had been the first to arrive at the meeting place in the Mexico City airport at the start of the week. Curiously, at that time, we unconsciously danced around each other for many minutes before directly approaching each other about being members of this pilgrimage group. It was as if we were animals in the wild, circling each other's presence, deciding to accept or reject our joint company. Well, we accepted each other at the airport, and we accepted each other at this pyramid site. The Voice was bringing us together for this singularly spectacular moment of the week.

We sat on the ground with my arms encasing her body from behind. She felt tense and later said that she was aware of her tension. As a wordless sign to her to relax, I moved my left hand from her wrist to under her left elbow. Silently, I asked her to relax, let go, release yourself from this tension. Well, what she released was much more than tension. I felt as if a bolt of lightning had shot from her body and right through mine. I had loosely used those words before (*felt like I had been struck by a bolt of lightning*), but never had this statement been truer than this powerful bolt released from her. From a balanced sitting position, my body was thrust by the bolt, and I hit the ground. People gathered around as I regained my faculties. I said to her that I thought that something had come out of her and through me. She said that she sensed the same as she felt my pain and simultaneously felt a great flood of release. I suggested to her that she pay attention to what comes to her over the next few days, because it seemed as though something very special was going on for her. She took her turn comforting me with both hands holding the place of entry of the lightning bolt. Then we stood and hugged and continued on with the day, both more than a bit mystified by the experience.

In a strange way, nothing about the rest of the day went the same for me as had occurred in the prior days of this week in Teotihuacan. I felt invisible and alone in many respects and just floated through the remainder of the day. The next morning I met up with her during breakfast. We spoke of the prior day's moment, and she shared that for the first time since her husband's passing, she felt unconditionally loved. Wow!! This is the moment!! Not only was she allowed and encouraged by the Voice to let go or release the grief that she held onto so tightly, but she was simultaneously given the truly comforting hug of unconditional love from the Divine. Wow!! All that I can say is, "Wow!!" This is exactly what the Voice, through the energies of Teotihuacan, was saying. "Let go, release, and feel the true love that is here for you." It was love, pure and simple, and unconditional. It was the energy of Teotihuacan flowing with perfection. It was there for us to witness, to witness and share. It was not a momentary phenomenon but a lasting memory to be shared generation after generation, the way the Toltecs told their love stories. It was the Voice that I had journeyed to Teotihuacan to hear, to witness and to bring back to you, my friends.

In Conclusion

Inspired by devotion, pilgrimages can truly be journeys to the most sacred places. Once in the sacred space, the Voice clearly has something very special for us to hear and share. The candle-lit labyrinth singing with the Voice reminding us to be the Voice in our own lives. The mind-to-mind flow of deep insights from teacher to student remind us that conversation and communication can go way beyond the limited realm of the linear world. And the lightning bolt message that captures our attention and truly reminds us to let go or release painful memories and accept the unconditional love that is here to take its place. All were powerful illustrations of what Divinity has for us, if only we will take the time to listen to the Voice.

Reflections With The Buddha

The Buddha demonstrated to us the life of a pilgrim as he left his comfortable abode, much to his family's early disappointment and headed out in search of the end of suffering for us all. Many now search for ways to honor the Buddha's selfless generosity by pilgrimaging to sites that he is said to have visited.

From the verse called "The Saint," is written,

Like the flight of birds in the sky, the path of the selfless is hard to follow. They have no possessions, but live on alms in a world of freedom. Like the flight of birds in the sky, their path is hard to follow. With their senses under control, temperate in eating, they know the meaning of freedom. (Easwaran, 1985, p. 133)

Most people, who set out on pilgrimage, do so with dedication and devotion in mind. These are not vacations or luxurious travels. The Buddha might well be proud to see us making the efforts. However, we know that these trips are short lived. We stay a week or so and then return to our normal daily lives. In order to truly benefit from these sacred journeys, it is important that we bring something back, something that stays with us and changes our lives. Having done so, we can know that we are heading towards our ultimate freedom.

From the verse called, "The Awakened One," comes thoughts on fear, "Driven by fear, people run for security to mountains and forests, to sacred spots and shrines. But none of these can be a safe refuge, because they cannot free the mind from fear" (Easwaran, 1985, p. 170). I sense that the Buddha is warning us against relying solely on these trips to end the suffering that we fear. The pilgrimage is not meant to be the miracle cure, but rather, the indication to ourselves that we mean to be free. We are willing to sacrifice in our present life for the ultimate freedom that can be ours. The Voice seems more encouraging in Its guidance, direction and support along these lines. The Voice seems to say, "Make the effort and you will be free; show your devotion and you will find freedom. Speak with Me, and I will guide you. Just listen and live in freedom."

CHAPTER 7

Voyages into Past Lives

▲▲▲

I EMBARKED ON MANY VOYAGES into past-lives over the last several years. What started out as a spiritual curiosity turned quickly into a knowingness that past-life work is a healing modality that is to be expanded to its fullest and shared broadly with humanity. The Voice has made quite clear to me that by the grace of God, we can see and relive our past incarnations to aid us through our current lives. Furthermore, the Voice made it even clearer to me that I was to investigate and share with humanity what is so very special about this seemingly forgotten gift of healing.

The question naturally arises, "Is this real or merely my imagination?" Because so many have forgotten the power of this gift, it seems that humanity, as a whole, thinks past-life visions are nonsensical dreams or imaginative hallucinations, or anything but reality. However, one does not have to dig too deeply into the recorded history of honored intellectual and spiritual beings to find rational beliefs in reincarnation and previous incarnations.

Elizabeth Clare Prophet, in her book, *Reincarnation, the Missing Link in Christianity* (1997), did a masterful job of researching and sharing the known history of beliefs stretching back from Neanderthal times through the middle ages, all the way to present day thinking. Her research not only shared forgotten facts, but also provided contextual footings for the times, as these beliefs were known to be commonplace.

Warren Jefferson, in his book, *Reincarnation Beliefs of North American Indians* (2008), researched and shared the sacred beliefs of the North American Indians. Rather than regurgitating their thoughts, let me encourage you to read their writings and find for yourselves how interwoven the concepts of reincarnation and past-lives were to many civilizations all around the globe and all throughout human time. When you are through reading these and other researcher's findings, you are likely to feel as I do, that it is much harder to not believe than it is to believe.

A follow-up question might naturally come to mind. If these concepts were so commonplace in societies all around the world and all throughout time, then why have we forgotten them so? Well, it is sad to say, but organized religions have done a pretty good job in purging and squashing these very concepts. Alongside reincarnation sat the belief that one could speak directly with God. This too was originally a commonly held belief. But, without thinking too hard, we can imagine how threatened organized religions must have felt with the idea that their intermediations were not all that necessary, and that souls might have multiple chances to progress along the spiritual path to their heavenly destinations.

With a little digging, we can discover that during the fourth and fifth centuries, before the great splintering of Christianity into so many separate languages and interpretations, the Roman Church came down extraordinarily hard on these concepts and replaced them with an even greater emphasis on Original Sin, fear, guilt, damnation and the possibilities of salvation through its intermediation. Century after century and to this day, many segments of organized religion continue to pound us with these mental pictures, loaded with fear and guilt, as opposed to offering us the liberation that naturally comes with our direct connection to God and the opportunities to progress along the path throughout our many lifetimes.

What I am hearing from the Voice is that enough is enough! The time has come to put an end to these ridiculous notions that God is not available to us, and that we should wallow in energies of fear and guilt, and that we only get one chance to get it right. The Voice has spoken the Truth to us through prophets, mystics, sages and teachers. I am certain that the Voice is speaking through me on these crucial concepts right now. I feel humbly blessed to have this Truth in my awareness, and I am so grateful to be able to share this with you through this very writing.

BEGINNING MOMENTS ON A SPIRITUAL CRUISE

I engaged with the Voice on many occasions in this regard, and the callings came to me in many layers. After twenty-five very successful years in the financial services industry and having completed my master's degree in education, leading me to a college-math teaching career, which I had expected to last indefinitely, I found myself faced with a very important decision. This was during the month of July, and I had received an invitation to be on a spiritual cruise, loaded with many popular spiritual teachers.

I had not been and still am not a big fan of cruises. However, I felt drawn to attend this spiritual cruise, in spite of the fact that it would occur during the following spring teaching semester. I could not teach and attend the cruise at the same time. I was called to make a choice that I had not expected, but in the end, truly appreciated. I received clearance from my school to take the spring semester off, which opened the door to an incredible time of spiritual study and soul-stimulation, in addition to joining the cruise with my wife.

One of the prominent spiritual teachers on this cruise was a man named Dr. Brian Weiss. He was, to my understanding, the foremost authority on past-life regression. A scientifically minded psychiatrist, graduated *magna cum laude* from Columbia University with a medical degree and serving as chief resident at Yale University, having published dozens of scientific-based articles on psycho-pharmacology, brain chemistry, sleep disorders, depression, anxiety and much more, he stumbled upon the past life of one of his patients during therapy. Dr.

Weiss had investigated and written several books on this topic for more than thirty years by the time of our cruise.

How we had heard of Dr. Weiss was another fascinating whispering in my ear by the Voice. My wife and I had attended the annual fundraiser for our local symphony orchestra where my wife sings in the chorus, and one of the silent auction items was a past-life regression session for two. Much to our surprise, we were the only ones to bid on this item, and so the session was ours. Neither of us knew anything about past-life regression, so we went to the internet and discovered the name of Dr. Weiss. A bit apprehensive about this session, we decided not to go to the silent auction person, but to select someone who had studied under Dr. Weiss to be our first guide. The Voice directed us to a truly marvelous and talented woman by the name of Susan Wisehart, who would take us on our very first voyage into past lives. Coming out of this first past-life vision, I felt "bitten by the bug." I returned for several more sessions before receiving the invitation to the spiritual cruise. Needless to say, seeing Dr. Weiss' name on the speaker list made my decision to attend the cruise that much easier.

The day with Dr. Weiss on this cruise brought powerful insights to me, and even more powerful emotional release to my wife. After arriving back home, I went to his website and came across an upcoming weeklong course at the Omega Institute in upstate New York. Without giving it a second thought, I signed up for and attended this intensive, designed to assist therapists in guiding clients into their past lives. Though I did not have clients, I did have interest in seeing and experiencing this powerful healing modality.

The training came second nature to me, and many powerful experiences occurred during this week with Dr. Weiss. In fact, the week was so sacred and powerful that I had real difficulty making my way home. Probably should not have been allowed to drive a car to the airport, navigation was tough, and I almost boarded on the wrong airplane as everything was a bit of a blur. By the way, if we are wondering if the Voice was truly speaking to me in this regard, all we have to do is look at the names of the key characters in my past-life guidance and training, Weiss and Wisehart. Need I say more?

Process Of Past Life Regression

Before we go any further, let me take a moment to describe what a past-life regression session is like. There are really three steps common to every session that I have been through, as either the guide or the guided.

First Step.

The first step is a bit of a warm-up conversation between the guide and the guided. The warm-up time allows the two to get acquainted, relieves possible anxieties, sets the stage for what is about to transpire, and importantly, gives the guide a sense of how receptive the guided might be. It is helpful for the guide to know to what extent the guided has familiarity with his or her unconscious mind through modes like meditation, contemplation, dreamwork, altered states, etc.

Second Step.

The second step is the actual voyage. Different guides use different techniques to bring the guided from the conscious state to the unconscious state where all of the important memories of this lifetime and previous lifetimes are stored. Mild hypnosis is used to allow these two minds to be in gear at the same time. So mild is the hypnosis that the guided definitely knows where he or she is, and can hear sounds from outside the session room.

I like to introduce a beautiful ray of light that the guided imagines coming into the crown of his or her head and flows through to every cell of his or her body. This brings a warm, tingling, energetic sensation that feels quite good and helps keep the guided feeling safe and alert. I then count down numbers to support a calm and peaceful, disposition. I then ask the guided to imagine walking down a staircase or riding down an escalator, which helps him or her to go deeper inside the unconscious. The guided then arrives in a garden of his or her own personal creation, allowing for trees, flowers, meadows, creeks, ponds or waterfalls, gentle loving animals, aromas and gentle breezes, anything and everything that supports peaceful, loving sensations and allows the focus on deep-seeded memories to come forth. Each garden contains a walking bridge that crosses some form of running water and connects this life to some life from the past.

When the guided feels rested and ready from time in the garden, I ask them to walk across this bridge as I count from five to one. When they step off the bridge on the other side of the water, they are in their past life and are asked to begin describing it to me. I must interject here that guiding is not about directing the guided through the life. The guide does not see or create any of the images of the life, but merely listens to the story of the guided. Through careful listening, the guide is more able to help the guided keep things moving from one important life moment to the next. There is quite a balance to maintain between allowing ample time in any particular life moment and moving the guided on to the next important moment.

THIRD STEP.

All of my sessions end with taking the guided to the deathbed scene and eventually into the light, where some time can be spent in the love of the celestial realm. We then return to the garden and then back to the room where we are sitting. Once fully back in the conscious mind, we tackle step three, which is a downloading conversation of what the guided saw and felt, and what connections these experiences might have to his or her current life.

The guide is usually a bit exhausted while the guided is generally full of energy. The guided shares what he or she considers to be the meaning of the visions and experiences, while the guide encourages expansion of these powerful thoughts and images.

The guided is advised to write out everything that he or she can remember of the time in the past life and celestial realm and then allow more to come over the subsequent days. Oftentimes, more information comes through the Voice that fills in gaps or blanks. The story expands to its fullest intention. This writing by the guided is mostly to allow for the continuation of the wisdom flow that emanates from the session. It is not needed to keep a record of the past life, because, different from a dream, the past life is not going to be forgotten. I can assure you of that.

Skeptics and those who just do not want to believe in past lives suggest that we just make these stories up, that it is all in our imaginations. Well, that could be true, except that I have never come across a past-life story that matched, in any way, the expectations of mine or anyone else that traveled into a past life.

Voyages Into Past Life Regression

If the imagination theory were accurate, then many male past-life travelers might expect to see themselves in heroic or dashing lives like gladiators, pirates, legendary heroes, etc.

First Regression.

My very first voyage into a past life was definitely none of the above, not even close. When asked what I looked like, I responded that I was a dark haired, dark eyed, tanned skin, young girl of about eight or nine years old. I had the sense of both viewing and being this young girl at the same time. This was definitely not what I might have expected; and yet, it felt very natural. When asked where I was,

I responded that I was walking along the beach with my parents and holding my mother's hand. As you will see, this was not a particularly long life story, but it certainly caught my attention. Before I knew it, I had let go of my mother's hand and was walking into the water. I just kept walking. First, I was in the water. Next, I was one with the water. I had the sense that I was never coming back to the life with these parents. I sensed their sadness and heard their cries. Yet, I felt calm, peaceful and very much at home in these new (or perhaps old) surroundings. I had the sense that I had let go of one mother's hand and grabbed onto another's. One mother now seemed temporary and the other now seemed more permanent.

This was a most unusual maiden voyage into the past-life world. As I said, it very much caught my attention. Considering how the Voice speaks with me, it seems as though it was more of an invitation into the realm of past-life discovery rather than a viewing of an actual past life. Yet, something inside says to me that it might have served both purposes, the viewing of a powerful past-life moment and being called to investigate further.

The powerful message coming through the Voice, to me, is that there is such a thing as this temporary life and such a thing as the permanent life. Many have pondered this question since the beginning of time. The Voice seems to be telling us, quite directly through this short story, that there is life after life. That while both are real and both can be pleasant and loving, one is temporary and the other is permanent. This calls us to look further and do what we can in the temporary life to prepare for what lies ahead in the permanent.

Second Regression.

The second time through a past life did not come to be any more expected than the first time in this realm. I found myself in an urban setting. It seemed to be a European city back in the seventeen hundreds. It was a very fast paced viewing of my life. I was already an adult man and very much in love with a woman. I was not positive whether she was my girlfriend, fiancé or wife. As it turned out, it did not really matter to the story.

All of a sudden, we were in an awful scene where she stabbed a man. It was not clear to me why she had done so, but before I knew it, the police were there, and she was about to be taken away. Without a moment's hesitation, I said to the officer that it was I who had stabbed the man to death in contradiction to what the eyewitnesses had reported. The officer asked me to repeat what I had said, and so I said again that it was I, not my wife, who had killed this man.

As I am writing these words, the word wife just came through my fingers, so, I guess that I did know at the time that she was my wife. In any event, the officer did not care who killed the man. One of us was going to face the consequences, and it was fine with him if that person was me. So, off to jail I went. You might be saying to yourself, "Hey man, this is just a hero's story that you are sharing with us." Well, as it unfolds further, I can assure you that I am not stroking my ego with grand thoughts of chivalry.

Next, I felt the aloneness of the prison cell, and that really hit hard. The guide asked me how I felt about what would likely happen to me. I responded that if one of us was going to be put to death, I would rather it be me than my wife, as I loved her so, and that I had no second thoughts or regrets about my instinctive decision. However, I was not prepared for the next scene. There I was, being marched to the area where the guillotine was sitting. It was in a barren courtyard and no one was there but my executioners and me. There was no crowd of onlookers as we have seen in movies like *Braveheart* or stories like "Joan of Arc." There was just an immense feeling of loneliness, and worst of all, there was no wife there to witness or support me in this, my last moment of this lifetime. That cut me harder than the blade that ended this life. However, the Voice was there to comfort me.

The Voice reminded me that my life is important, and that there is nothing wrong with heroism, just to be mindful of what you are here to do and give up this life only for the deepest of reasons. Find your happiness within and share your life with others. But, most of all, do not ever think that you are actually alone. The loneliness feeling is definitely a delusion, for we are truly never ever alone.

Third Regression.

As a frame of reference, I would say that I went back for a new past-life regression about every six months or so. I went to the same guide each time because she was talented and gave me some consistency in my discovery. The third past-life story was about a year after the first and started out more in tune with what a man might dream of seeing and being. As I crossed the bridge into this past life, I saw myself as a young man, riding on a magnificent horse with a beautiful woman riding at my side. This was taking place somewhere in medieval times. The path was lined on both sides with cheering people, voicing a hero's welcome home of sorts. We were heading in procession to a splendid castle up the hill, and the feelings inside me were enormous.

The next scene took place inside this castle. The view was twofold in that I seemed to be peeking through a keyhole at a wedding scene in a church loaded with people, but the closer that I looked the more it seemed that I was the protagonist that I was looking at. So, there I was, standing at the altar with a royal minister and my beautiful bride to be. The next scene was that of the consummation of the marriage and quickly came the news that a royal son had just been delivered to my world. "OK," you say, "This is the dream-like imagination that skeptics were talking about." I urge you to stay tuned to what comes ahead. Not only was I young, handsome, royal, married to a beautiful queen with an heir to my throne, but, the villagers loved me. I saw myself in their presence sharing the wealth of the kingdom with them. I walked among the villagers passing out loaves of bread and cheese. And now you are saying to yourself, "Come on dreamer, this is a dream."

Well, I left my entourage and kept walking along the path that led beyond the village to a forest-like setting. Suddenly an eerie, very dark feeling came over me. Before I could make sense of the feeling, I found myself being stabbed from all sides by men who had been hiding in the forest. It was as unpleasant a feeling as you might imagine. It was not so much pain from the swords as it was the pain from who held the swords.

My guide asked if I recognized these four men from my current life. The closer that I looked, the surer I was that I did know these men in both lifetimes. That was an eye opener for me. An instantaneous connection came to me about the men in this current lifetime. They all seemed to be competing with me, and in their own ways, they seemed to be envious of me.

This realization did not bring a comfortable feeling to me, but it did bring some better understanding of my relationships with these four men. After some time of serious reflection regarding this past life, and particularly its ending, I decided to reach out to these men, individually and one at a time. I did not share my past-life story with them, but just became a bit more involved in their lives. I guess that you could say that my past-life realization about this life brought a feeling of unconditional love for these men. By reaching out to them, I was undoing the leftover need on their parts to continue to be envious of me. In an unspoken way, I was saying that what is mine is yours as well. Let us enjoy our life together rather than continuing the problems of the past life. And, do you know what? It worked. The envious or competitive feelings that I noticed before the past-life session seemed to disappear.

That is an important message that I hear consistently from the Voice when it comes through past-life work. The Voice seems to be saying, "Have a look at this moment or series of moments from your past life and see that there is no need to bring those harmful or limiting feelings into this lifetime. That life is over. Let go and move on with what is important for this life."

GUIDING OTHERS IN PAST LIFE REGRESSION

In case you think that these stories involve stretching for meaning, let me share one that requires no slack whatsoever. Mariia is a cute young Ukrainian girl who was in her very early twenties when I met her. She was care giving to Florence, the lovely lady that I met with on Thursdays. It was summertime, and I mentioned that Mariia was fortunate because the local swimming pool was just a few blocks from the house in which the two women lived. She said that she was deathly afraid of water and would not be going to the pool as she does not go to the beach or lakes or any type of water playground. I thought that was unfortunate for such a young person to be unable to enjoy water in so many ways.

Nonetheless, Mariia joined our conversations each Thursday and was particularly interested in hearing about past lives. After about six months of Thursdays, she asked if I would take her into a past life. I suggested that she practice meditating for a month or so, and then we would try it. She agreed and raised the question again after a month of practice.

Mariia was easily guided into the past life of a fighter pilot. Her descriptions matched very closely my memories of the movie, "Top Gun." Sometime after the session I asked if this particular movie was one of her favorites. She quickly responded that she had never seen or heard of this movie. She was probably too young.

No matter, in this past life she was male (which is not unusual for different genders to pop up) and spoke fluent English (which was remarkable for me to hear, as English is definitely not her normal language in this current lifetime).

As in all the past lives that I take people through, we ended up at the death seen, and I asked her to describe where she was and what was happening.

Much to my amazement, she said that she was at the bottom of a lake, and that she was drowning. I quickly suggested that she float above her body (no pun intended) and just watch the final moments before heading into the celestial realms. She was not afraid, and took her time through the process.

After the session, during our reflection conversation, I suggested that we go to my health club soon to try out the swimming pool. My experience had told me that having drowned in the past life was a legitimate reason to be fearful of water, but that was in the past life and not necessary to carry forward into this current lifetime. Furthermore, having seen her own drowning in the past life, she was now aware of the cause of her fear.

Mariia reluctantly agreed to come with me to the pool for she is a brave young woman in every other way but the fear of water. Within two short swim sessions she was swimming like a fish, on her back, on her stomach, head in, head out, without any help from me. Suddenly, she realized what she was doing and became extremely excited. She hurried home to call her mother to tell her that she was swimming!! You might say, "Swimming, what's the big deal?" But, I assure you that if you had seen the terror on her face about swimming before you saw her swim, you would know exactly what I am talking about. In the end, I did not have to interpret anything for Mariia. The Voice spoke directly to her saying. "Fear not the water; enjoy the water; teach your future children to enjoy the water."

Even though Mariia drowned in the past life, she enjoyed the memories of the life. I must say, most people have done the same. They may have fears, in advance, usually that they might have been a bad person, but that rarely ever comes up. Mostly, we get to see ways in which we can make alterations to our current ways of seeing the life that we are leading. Only one time did I feel the need to stop a session and bring someone back before they had finished the past-life viewing. She was a friend of a friend whom I had never met. So, we needed to spend a bit of time getting acquainted. During our conversation she mentioned that she had made some rather drastic and positive changes in her life and her behaviors. She was not exactly sure why she wanted to see a past life, but felt called to do so. Well, as you are about see, she was in the right place at the right time.

We started out in her past-life childhood and worked forward for a while until she arrived at her adult self. We wandered a bit through this adult life until she came to a terrible place. She was having serious difficulty going on in this life. I originally hoped that things would clear up, but they did not. She was so uncomfortable that I made the decision to bring her out. She was grateful. She said that the him that she was in her past life, was such a bad person and was doing all the things, that in her current life, she had decided to discontinue doing. Well, there it is. The Voice was telling her that she had made the right decision about changing her current ways. This past-life viewing was meant to underscore and confirm just how important her recent life-altering decisions had been. This is very powerful stuff.

Only once have I encountered difficulty in guiding someone into a past life, and even that experience had the mighty Voice coming through loud and clear. This friend just could not seem to move forward. She seemed stuck in the garden and had trouble crossing the bridge. We tried and tried and finally I asked her if she could see a light. I had given up on the past life and was hoping that she might spend some time in the celestial realm. She said that she did see a light, and when prompted, she went straight into it. Once there, this rather skeptical person was greeted by angels and was treated to so much loving that she was holding herself and crying in this current body. They told her how much they loved her and were anxious to re-connect with her when she was through in this lifetime. I let her stay in the glorious place for quite a while before bringing her back to the room where we were sitting.

Once back in conversation, it came to us that in her current life she was stuck just like in the garden. She was having trouble making decisions and moving forward in ways that she knew that she needed to move. We noticed that her difficulty in the past-life session was highly correlated to the difficulties in her present life. The Voice was telling her to let go of her indecisiveness and keep moving. The angels had reminded her that she is worthy and ready to move forward. It was so clear that even this apparently unsuccessful past-life session was powerfully successful. It seems that if the Voice is speaking, and we are listening, something very important will come through. This is the truest gift of past-life work. We go to a place where we can disconnect the conscious mind and allow the unconscious to reveal the needed memories that are conveniently stored there. It is truly that simple. What calls us to this important point is, of course, the Voice!

GUIDING ONE'S SELF IN PAST LIFE REGRESSION

In addition to being taken into past lives and taking others into their past lives, I have occasionally taken myself into my own past lives. While the two former processes are quite easy and natural for me, the latter is always a bit challenging. It might be somewhat analogous to driving a car. It is not hard to be the driver or the passenger, but it is difficult being both at the same time. It is not all that easy or safe to drive and look out the side windows at the same time. Furthermore, when I take someone into a past life, the person has two very distinct voices. They have the voice of the present life person and the voice of the past-life person. Then, I, as guide, add a third voice. When I am taking myself into a past life, I am really all three voices. That is pretty hard to keep straight. The end result is that my solo voyages into my own past lives have tended to come more as fragments of information rather than free flowing streams of story. The visions were more like snapshots than running film. Still, the Voice did not seem to mind. Powerful messages came through the fragments.

The most memorable self-driven past life was of my time as a Lakota spiritual warrior. Visions of this life have actually come through several separate voyages. I have seen myself peacefully paddling a canoe along a river bordered on both sides by luscious tall fir trees. I have seen myself standing before groups of Lakota villagers. I have seen myself in battle, sometimes shooting arrows, and sometimes in vivid hand-to-hand combat. But, the most striking moment came during my pilgrimage to Sedona.

I had been to a favorite bookstore the day before this vision. I had purchased a couple of books on past lives, actually. When I got to the counter, I noticed a book about a particular Lakota warrior and without any clear thought, quickly grabbed it to take home as well. The day after the purchase I was deeply in a meditative place and decided to turn the moment into a past life.

Without much effort, I saw myself riding my horse along a riverbed, with thunder and lightning following us with powerful rumbling energies. There was a red-tailed hawk flying above us as we road like the wind through this scene. Painted markings on me and on my horse were quite visible.

I sensed two very powerful yet distinct feelings simultaneously. They were indestructibility and sadness. This scene was bigger than a fragment but smaller than a full-blown vision. It did have a flow that was sometimes fast paced and sometimes slow motion. Before I left this scene and life, I wanted to know my name. I really struggled with wanting and trying to come up with the name of myself in that life. I had seen this man so many times but never knew his name. Unfortunately, the name did not come to me while in this moment. I let go of that life and rejoined this one, more than a little bit disappointed.

The vision was the most powerful of this series of voyages to this life, but the name was still missing. You might be thinking, "Did not you say that just the day before you bought a book on a particular Lakota spiritual warrior? Why don't you just look at the book that you just bought?" Do not forget that my time in Sedona was very non-linear. What we might take as totally logical in the linear dimension does not fit the same in the non-linear realm.

Well, a couple of days later I did mindlessly open this book and began reading. I have to emphasize that I had never read about this particular man before. I had never ever heard what I am about to tell you.

So, I opened the book and began reading. The story was enjoyable, and I was taken in by its flow, when, all of a sudden I began seeing the words that I had just shared with you about my past life. The author was describing a vision that this spiritual warrior had had in his life. It was his most powerful vision brought on by a quest that he had prepared for by himself. Normally, a holy man would prepare one for the quest for a vision. But, this particular time, being the independent soul that he was, he just went off by himself in search of a vision. He surely received one, and so did I.

The horse riding, the thunder and lightning, the red-tailed hawk, the markings, and the reasons for the indestructibility and sadness became known to me. He was sure that he would never be killed by arrows or bullets in battle, but that his own people would some day take him down and end his life.

Reading these words was like a Twilight Zone moment for me. Out of a very deep place just a few days earlier I had seen something that had come out of a very deep place that he had been during his lifetime. More than surreal, this was incredibly striking to me, and caused quite a bit of reflection on my part. Fortunately, I was in a place that encouraged and supported reflection and understanding. I was in a place where the Voice was my constant companion.

Let us go back, for a moment, to the place where you were asking me why I did not just look at the book that I had purchased two days before. Well, to be perfectly honest, the conscious thought never actually occurred to me. You might say that that makes no sense, and I would agree. However, here is a key point about past-life work. Remember when we were talking about imagination and creating our own stories and believing that these were actual past lives. Well, it seems to me that the conscious mind and the unconscious mind are not as linked together as we might suspect. The conscious mind really had no idea with what the unconscious mind was so familiar. It seems as though the Voice was not about to interfere at that exact time. It seems that the most powerful moment came when I recognized the connection between my current life and this past life of mine. I see these past-life moments as true gifts from Divinity. I see them as unthinkable opportunities to peer into the past to assist us through the struggling times of our present lives. I sense that this particular past-life moment was the Voice telling me to be sure to tell you these very thoughts.

Multiple Visits To A Past Life: Expanding Consciousness

The last past-life that I want to share with you is my most recent past life. It is one that I have voyaged to on three different occasions with the help of my favorite guide, Susan Wisehart. We are about to see that each viewing is of the same life, but each viewing reveals more information and more understanding of this lifetime. It is as though the Voice is providing more expanded clarity each time through the regression.

First Voyage.

The first time through I crossed the bridge to find myself as a six-year-old boy with a father and mother and newly born brother. Mine appeared to be a very happy and loving family.

The next scene was set in a schoolroom where I was being beaten by the teacher for unknown reasons. I guess that they did a lot of that back in the day. I was eleven years old at the time.

The next scene had people in some kind of vehicle which seemed to crash. I found myself lifting people out of the vehicle with my parents killed and my brother badly injured. I saw myself carrying my brother along a dirt road to a doctor's office some distance away from the accident. This scene was followed by my watching a lot of activity and commotion in the doctor's office, with heavy anxiety and concern. I am not sure why, but I felt a strong sense of guilt. I sensed that I was about sixteen years old at the time. My emotions were building as my senses were bringing me a memory of a painful funeral scene. Having lost my family in a blink of an eye and being just a teenager at the time, I found myself as a monk in a monastery, praying for penance for whatever it was that brought the guilty feelings.

In the monastery I led a simple, peaceful life and left it with no regrets of any kind. On my deathbed, I felt that I was alone in my small room. I saw a light, but was not sure where it had come from, but before I knew what happened, I had gone into the light and was gone.

Second Voyage.

The second voyage into this same life brought me straight to the doctor's office. My emotions clicked in immediately, as I saw my little brother on an operating table. There was lots of commotion in the room, and before I knew it, they had covered the body of my newly deceased brother. Many tears were shed in both my past life and my current life.

The next scene was of me walking towards the monastery, admiring the big church and beautiful stone buildings. The scene was dark but beautiful as I gazed at the windows of this grand church. I walked with a sense that I was searching for something as I entered the monastic grounds. But, this time I felt happy and welcomed by the monks and others.

A big surprise came through this voyage as I saw that I was the one stand-ing on the altar, speaking to the church full of monks. Tremendous emotions flowed as I realized that I was the Abbot, and they were listening intently to what I was saying. Great serenity flowed through me as I noticed the light of the altar glowing in this mostly dark church setting. I was at peace and loved my life. On my deathbed, I noticed that many people filled my tiny room. I felt as though I had helped many in this lifetime and was content to move on. I noticed a light coming through my small window, went into the light, and in a flash, I was gone.

Third Voyage.

This third voyage began with my viewing of this same life beginning at the monastery. Clothed in a dark brown robe, I was already about forty years old. Asked by Susan what name do they call me, I responded Fr. Francis, and later refined that it François or Francesco. With strong hands and a medium build, I had skin that was weathered by my time in the fields. We worked the land as a self-supported community of equals with healthy camaraderie.

While I was Abbot, I was often in the fields with my fellow monks. Regarding the monastery's location, I saw mountains and forests surrounding our land, which seemed to be somewhere in Europe, with old stone buildings. The church is prominent in this scene. Queried by Susan about my leadership, I responded that I lead the group by example.

The next scene found me in a hospital building in the nearby town, which reminded me of an infirmary. It was not a big room with beds in two aisles. I was praying with the people in the beds. These people were not going to live much longer. I sensed that I was there to console them in the last days of their lives. I felt a very emotional loving connection to these people. Overwhelmed by empathy with the pain of the surviving family member, I felt their pain. I was there to bring them comfort; but, it took some toll on me.

The next scene was back at the monastery, back in the church. There was a really bright light all around me. It seemed out of place to me in this normally dark church. The light was not coming through a window. These rays of light seemed strange to me. I saw sparkly golden vestments all around me that did not seem right to me in a simple, country, mountain, self-supporting, working monastery.

As I tried to describe to Susan what I was seeing, the context just did not seem right to me. "What was this brilliantly powerful golden light doing in this place," I kept asking myself.

Let me say that the answers to this deeply meaningful question will definitely be answered when we get to the time between lives in our next chapter. I am not intentionally creating high drama here. The Voice does make this all very clear in the next chapter. However, I want you to know that, at this moment in the past life, I was feeling very perplexed, and you should get the idea that when viewing this and other past lives, I was as surprised by events as you might be. In other words, while I was the protagonist, I was also learning about the life as it was being shown to me. This was particularly evident to me in this past-life viewing.

The deathbed scene came next, and it started by my being amazed at how high the window was in my room. I remember saying that it seemed like twenty to thirty feet off the ground, and this was, again, out of context for this simple monastic setting. I was older. I was ill with many people in my room. I felt their sorrow for my loss much more than I felt my pain of leaving this life. My last words were to comfort them. This time my departure into the light came before I was asked about leaving. I was long gone into the light.

SIMILARITIES AND EXPANSIONS OF THE VOYAGES

I think that we can see the similarities of these descriptions of this life, but what stands out to me is how much more is shown as we went from first voyage to second voyage and incredibly more information was provided during the third voyage. It was curious to me to see what ages were my starting points in each voyage. Clearly, I started out older each lifetime. Additionally, we saw a changing context from a guilty penance-seeking monk seemingly dying alone in his small room developing into a much more empowered Abbot who loved his monks, served his community, and died in the company of many loving souls. I think that it is important from my experiencing these three voyages to say that it is not that the story changed, but rather that, what I was aware of and what I focused on expanded throughout these three voyages. Even how the light was described and how I entered the light was more expansive and understood the second and third time through the regression.

CONCLUDING THOUGHTS

We have covered an awful lot of water in these voyages to past lives, and the Voice clearly was with us the whole way. From the initial "bug" planted in my ear, to the cruise and training, to the many ways that I and others have learned valuable lessons about living this current life from the visions of prior lives, to the depth that came through multiple visits to the same past life. I hope that you sensed the sacredness that I felt all the way through these powerful moments. While the sessions may have provided enjoyment, they definitely were much more than entertainment. Valuable lessons were quickly learned that otherwise might have required years of weekly therapy appointments.

I may have failed to give proper emphasis on the sense of *déjà vu* that occurs following the past-life review session. My wife's session on the spiritual cruise cemented her lifelong connection to a past life that she led in China. All during my childhood, I felt almost insulted by the ways that Indians were portrayed by Hollywood and others in this country. The past-life visions of my Lakota heritage reconciled in my adult years what bothered me so much in my childhood years.

Finally, I have an uncle who is a Benedictine monk at a small working monastery in southern Indiana. He recently celebrated his fifty-year jubilee there. My family used to visit every so often. My brothers and sister never really liked going there, as it was Spartan and offered little means of entertainment, but I loved going there. The stone buildings and grand church, the darkness and sounds of the monks singing Gregorian chants, all contributed to a mystical feeling inside of me. I came very close to becoming a priest in this lifetime, but was talked out of it by a young Jesuit priest at just the right moment. I have been on several solitary retreats in this lifetime and each time I hear back from the Voice, "Your devotion is nice, now get back out into the world." We will find in the next chapter that I was not meant to repeat my monastic life, but to bring the message of the Voice to the larger human community.

REFLECTING WITH THE BUDDHA

The Buddha spoke of reincarnating many times but never truly offered much about his living those past lives. It seemed that he was so turned off by normal human existence in favor of the immortal life spent in nirvana.

From the verse called, "Age," we receive these thoughts, "This body is a painted image, subject to disease, decay and death, held together by thoughts that come and go. What joy can there be for those who see that their white bones will cast away like gourds in the autumn" (Easwaran, 1985, p. 150)? From this we hear that we are truly not the body, and that our existence is held together by our thoughts. The Buddha's advice is to ditch selfish human thoughts and hold onto selfless, yet blissful thoughts of nirvana. I must say that the Voice is giving me quite a bit more on the subject of human existence. The body, itself, is made of the identical substances of the physical universe, so, I honor it and the earth that we inhabit. The Voice is telling us to make the most of each lifetime, as they are each precious. Through our viewing of past lives, we might loosen the bindings that come from those past lives, where the context was different from this lifetime.

CHAPTER 8
Odysseys of Between Lives

▲ ▲ ▲

FAR AND AWAY THE MOST powerful and spectacular of these sacred journeys in search of the Voice is what I call the Odysseys of Between Lives. Having just voyaged into the realm of past lives, the Odyssey takes us, purely in soul form, into the place that the soul goes between these lives or incarnations. It is the very place where the soul reflects upon the activities, experiences of the past life, and then makes its preparations and sets its purposes and intensions for its next life inside the human form. It goes without saying, that once in this Divinely celestial place, we are truly in the most sacred of the sacred. We will see how directly and magnificently the Voice speaks to us and shows us how much we are loved and appreciated for the work that we do in the earthly or human realm.

My personal research took me three times into this mystical realm to see what the Voice had for me to bring back to you. Additionally, but only after experiencing for myself, I turned to the writings of noted spiritual scientists Dr. Michael Newton and Dr. Rudolf Steiner for comparison to the decades of research that they each had done. Dr. Newton, with a doctorate in counseling psychology, kept notes on thirty-five years of client between-life conversations before publishing his first book on the subject, went on to write several more books and broadens our understanding of the conversation that is available between guide and soul. Dr. Steiner studied mathematics, physics, chemistry and biology at the Vienna Institute of Technology and completed his doctorate in philosophy at the University of Rostock, Germany, before founding a spiritual movement called anthroposophy, which was his attempt to synthesize science with spirituality. Like the many thousands of cases that were collected, reviewed and shared with us by Dr. Raymond Moody in near-death experience and Dr. Brian Weiss in past-life regression, Newton and Steiner offered us scientifically rigorous compilations of experiences in the soul and celestial realm. It was comforting to me to see such strong similarities between the remarkable visions through the Voice to me and the cases described by these noted spiritual researchers.

As was the case in most of my personal past-life voyages, Susan Wisehart guided me into and through my personal between-life odysseys. Additionally, as I have guided many into and through many past lives, I have guided many into the spectacular celestial realm and into the very heart of the soul's experiences. I will describe much of what I saw and experienced as both the guide and the guided, and most importantly, spoken to us by the Voice.

SETTING A CONTEXT FOR THE ODYSSEYS

First, let me set a bit of context for our upcoming odysseys. The gateway into the odyssey of between lives was always from the vantage point of the past-life regression. There is abundant science in this route. Our conscious or waking mind is vibrating (most of the time) in the beta wave state. Our subconscious mind, where childhood and past-life memories are stored, is vibrating in the alpha wave state. Our superconscious mind, where the soul stores its memories, is in the theta wave state. You might remember my telling Mariia, before my taking her into a past-life, to spend a month practicing meditation. Her practicing meditation allowed her mind to practice noticing the different states that would be gone through on its way to the past-life memories.

The most direct route to the soul memories is from the conscious or beta wave state to the subconscious or alpha wave state and on to the super-conscious or theta wave state. So, it is very helpful to the process to spend some time in the most recent past-life before going through the light into the celestial realm. It has been my experience that we actually transmigrate from the deathbed into the light, and then, into the celestial realm. The amount of hypnotic prep work that Susan did with me, and I did with others, was highly correlated to the desired state of the final destination, which was deep for past-life, human memories and even deeper for soulful, between-life memories.

The guided needs to stay focused in a past-life regression for sixty to ninety minutes, while three to four hours might be required for the combination past-life and between-life viewing. You might say that that is a lot of work for the guided person. In truth, the guided pretty much skates through it, as time to them is meaningless, while the guide works his or her" tail off." Again, it is not that the guide is setting the direction as much as it is moving the person or soul along the path of memories and keeping the guided soul's focus straight, so he or she can see what they want and are intended to see.

CELESTIAL MOMENTS

Let me describe a few lighter celestial moments before going into the full-blown between-life sessions with you. At the end of each past-life viewing, as the person is seeing himself or herself on his or her deathbed, I tell the person to hover above the body, then I ask if the person can see a light. If so, I tell he or she to go into that light. They always see the light and always go into it (and by the way, to skeptics of the out-of-body phenomenon, they always hover over the deathbed body as if it were the most natural thing to be doing, with absolutely no help from me).

Once in the light, they are approached by soul guides, angels, teachers and, or departed loved ones. Often times, the loved one is particularly special to this person and is allowed to converse in real time with them. This is a truly Divine gift to cross the perceived barriers between these two dimensions. Wisdom is shared, tears flow, and a feeling of unconditional love is shared between the two souls.

A dear friend of mine's mother had passed away a couple of years prior to my taking her into a past life. While she enjoyed the past-life viewing, she really perked up during her time in the light. She had been worried about her deceased mother and thought that she left with hard feelings or unfinished business between them. Once in the light, her mother presented herself in all her celestial glory and made it quite clear to her daughter that she need not worry, and that there was nothing but unconditional love between them, no hard feelings, no unfinished business. It was quite clear that the mother was totally aware of her daughter's thoughts and concerns from the celestial realm. As an added bonus, the mother told her daughter that they could continue their conversation any time that the daughter so desired. She mentioned a few things about the daughter's two daughters, which were surreal for the daughter to hear, and then vanished into thin air.

My friend, the daughter, came out of this session a wholly different person. She was relieved about her mother, aware of her mother's continued aliveness, touched by their lasting connection and overwhelmed by the unconditional love that flowed between them.

Where was the Voice in all of this? Well, I would say that it was the Voice who orchestrated the timing of the viewing of this past-life session in order to allow the celestial visit between the daughter and her mother. The wisdom that flowed through the daughter's new understandings were clearly from the Voice, and told her that her mother was still alive in the celestial realm and aware of her daughter's concerns. The unconditional love shared between the two was likely presented through the Voice. It revealed that enough worry time on the part of the daughter had passed and needed extinguishing, so that she could move on with her life and be the best mother that she was intended to be for her own two daughters. Just think, all of this transpired inside a ninety-minute block of linear time.

A different dear friend of mine asked me to take her into a past life. We went through all of the warm-up steps, and as she crossed the bridge into what was intended to be a past-life, we found her in a state of awareness that had no body, time or sense of limited space. She knew that she was there, but there was no body and there was no place. A very strong connection from her departed father came through to her and she enjoyed his presence without his physical form. At the same time there was a connection to an animal totem, that of a wolf. Her father and the wolf held strong connections to her, and she seemed to know that she had devoutly followed them both when called to do so. She knew that she had been a good follower, but she was about to learn that she was also a good leader.

The next scene in her celestial visit took place in a very far away and sacred space. The friend saw herself as a light within a channel that reached many lights. She heard from the Voice that she had a voice that connected to all of these lights and that she was to continue to communicate intended messages to them. Naturally, she felt honored to be holding this position in the celestial realm. There was no ego attached to this feeling, far from it. She felt great reverence and humility to be where she was and doing what she was doing. Incidentally, the purpose that this friend always felt in this current lifetime was to teach. She has spent many decades joyfully doing just that.

The friend came back to the garden and back to the sitting room. She connected the celestial concepts, given by the Voice, to her current life. Not only was she reminded of her love for her father, but, she sensed the meaning of why she felt so connected to her friends here on earth. They were truly at the soul level. The time in the celestial realm reminded her of things that her conscious, human mind was not so aware. She was reminded of her leadership abilities and responsibilities in this lifetime as in the celestial realm. Who but the Voice would take the time to bother to remind her of these important and personal concepts.

As I said earlier, all of the past lives that I guided people through, ended with celestial visits. I would say that the past-life viewing was the cake, and the celestial visit was the icing. The Voice was the baker, and I stirred the ingredients.

Personal Odysseys into the Celestial Realm

First Odyssey.

My first, full-blown odyssey into between lives, as I said earlier, was guided by Susan Wisehart. She had taken me into several past lives, and we were quite comfortable with one another. Trust and comfort in the guide and guided relationship is mandatory for a successful odyssey, in my view. Of course, the Voice was clearly the most important element of this experience.

Susan had suggested that I might encounter guides, teachers, fellow members of my soul group, and most likely the Council of Elders. These were all beings that she was aware of both from personal experience as a guide and a guided soul, and also learned about while studying under Dr. Newton.

Right off the bat, as I entered the light, I was greeted by my long-standing personal guide. John is his name, Joshua is mine at this soul level, so I was told. As I quickly learned, John has been with me through many, many lifetimes and between lives. His aura was as pure as the driven snow. His manner was confidently compassionate, wise and loving. His appearance was with white haired, white bearded, white flowing robe. John was whiter than white and radiated wisdom and patience that only Divine seasoning on earthly and celestial realms can produce. I felt fortunate and honored to have John as my guide.

In our initial conversation, I learned from John that I was and have always been a loyal servant of God. He said that in this past life as the Abbot of the mountain monastery, I had done very good work, and that when I was ready to return to the earthly realm, I would be asked to do this same work, but this time outside of the monastic setting, out in the world.

This revelation goes a very long way in my understanding of why I might have felt drawn to the monastic life and almost chose the priestly vocation. However, as we can see here, I was not meant to repeat this lifestyle and was very timely discouraged from doing so by the Jesuit advisor at the end of my freshman year of high school. Do we suppose that the Voice had something to do with this powerful message given to me at a most impressionable age?

John then brought me to two highly dramatic vistas with a sacred forest in between. The first vista displayed crystal mountains, rolling hills and valleys with shimmering rivers. I heard myself say how beautiful and natural it appeared. It was a splendid site. Next, he ushered me to the second vista, which was the earth in its most pristine way, with mountains and valleys, rolling hills and rivers to behold. Again, I commented on its natural beauty.

It did not occur to me until after the session how these two very differently textured visions of similar sites produced the same exclamation from me. How could these radically different visions, one crystalline and one earthly, both garner the same refrain from me? I might suggest that this is a very important message from the Voice coming through to us here. We are to know that both the earthly life and celestial life come with unspeakable natural beauty. I might also comment that Dr. Newton often heard in his research of crystal mountains appearing in the celestial realm.

John then sat me down on a comfortable rock inside the dark, lush forest. Sitting on the rock, I felt that I was supposed to prepare myself for my upcoming life, out in the world. I felt that I was there to get myself ready. I began meditating to gather the wisdom inside and to center myself for the life ahead. The Voice told me that I do not have a lot of preparatory work to do. Next, I heard the Voice say that David is here to help you in your coming life.

David, the Sedona teacher that I have referred to in this current life, appeared to me in a holographic way. I heard myself say that he is *Real*, he is here and there, that his spirit is helping me and will guide me in my current life. I have to interject that this startled me greatly. It came as such a pleasant surprise that David was supposed to be in my current life. You might say, "Of course, you have been studying and visiting him for years now." However, I tell you once again that this came as a very pleasant surprise to me in the celestial realm. It brought me a true sense of relief that the teacher that I was following was the intended teacher from before this life began.

A long pause took place before what I thought would be a visit with my next guide. John had come, and David had come. I was looking forward to my next visitor. I sat patiently and all of a sudden the vision of Jesus Christ came to me in the forest. First it was the form, and then it was the Light, a very, very bright white light took over my senses. I was very confused and kept thinking that this should not be happening. It was too good, I heard myself say several times.

The loving energy that I was surrounded by and engulfed in was extraordinary. The feeling is hard to describe, but the closest that I can come to is that it is like floating in a sea of pure love. I cried, and I know that Susan cried, as the loving light filled both the forest and the room in which she and I were sitting.

I heard myself say many times that I am not worthy. But each time, the Voice of Jesus kept responding, "Worthy."

This time in the light with Jesus brought such a feeling of incredible humility to me. It then seemed as though I travelled back and forth into the light in the room of my deathbed. The light that brought me out of the human realm and into the celestial realm was this same light that I was swimming in with Jesus. Then I heard Him say, "Teach Love." This was a powerfully clear message. Then more words came, "You did well, and We want you to do more." I sensed that returning to the earthly plane was my choice, but that I was wanted to return for this reason. I heard myself say, "I will return. I am happy to do so."

After some joyfully tearful time passed, Susan asked if I was ready to move on. As much as I wanted to stay, I heard myself say, "Yes." She then asked if there was anyone else, besides David, that would be assisting me in the current life. I saw a hologram of my wife, Cheryl, and me. I sensed that she was in this life to help me and support me in my teaching love. I sensed that our partnership would serve dual purposes: mine as Divine teacher, and hers as Divine supporter. Anyone who has ever met Cheryl knows her to be a masterful and unconditional supporter. She is the ultimate Florence Nightingale, not in a nursing way, but in a supporting way. It is not surprising to me that the moment we met in this lifetime, we seemed to be surrounded by a mystical swirling energy of love, connection and purpose.

That was the end of my first odyssey of between lives. Susan and I went over the events that transpired and connected to meaningful moments in this lifetime. I would say that most of what I learned and connected was pretty self evident from what I have just described to you. It was really about discovering the love that God has for me, and the purpose of this lifetime: I am to teach love. Further, that I am being assisted by John, David and Cheryl, to name a celestial few.

Finally, the concept of timing of this visit comes to mind, similarly to the timing of past-life viewing. It seemed awfully strange to be seeing and hearing conversations that actually took place before I was born, viewing them in the middle of my life span that they are honoring. The Voice seems to be saying that the chronological linear time element that seems so natural to us human beings, is really an illusion, and not so in the celestial space. The soul is truly timeless in a most non-linear way.

SECOND ODYSSEY.

We are about to enter the sacred space of my second odyssey. As I listen to the recording of my second odyssey of between lives and reflect upon the notes that I took following it, I clearly see similarities to the first odyssey, but I also see more expanded views and differing points of emphasis from the Voice. As I de- scribe this second odyssey, I will point out some of the most important vantage points.

We started out in the same life, actually at my brother's funeral. This time, though, I did not feel any sense of guilt or responsibility for his passing. After all, the whole family and others had crashed and many died. How could that have been my doing? The Voice wanted to clear that unnecessary sense of personal guilt from my memory bank, it seems.

Next, I entered the monastery. This time I saw myself walking proudly with intentions to make something happen there, as opposed to just ending up there, due to the loss of my family. I definitely went there as part of my life's purpose. This time through, it was hard to miss that I had been the Abbot, the leader of the monastic community. The life seemed much more rewarding than the first view of it. I now understand that the life was not solitary, not alone. I lived and died in the loving company of this monastic family.

This second time through, I was aware of the light in the deathbed room and that I "shot through the dark, soaring through the light." Next, I was aware that I had arrived in a mystical garden setting with shimmering dust in the air and on the ground. This garden had a circular marble bench with a kind of throne-like backing in the middle, where I was sitting. I say sitting, as if I had a body, which of course I did not, but it was as if I was sitting on the bench with the throne backing to lean against. I heard myself say that I was a little tired, and I guess that I was there to rest.

I heard a noise coming from bushes very near to where I was sitting. I looked over to see a group of cherub-like kids peeking through the bushes, trying to get a glimpse of the new guy—me. This made me chuckle with joy as I sensed that my arrival was something special to these joyful youngsters. As I am writing these words, I am reminded of the joyful, playful animals that appeared in my vision quest at dusk.

Next came what Dr. Newton and Susan call the Council of Elders. There is a kind of path, not on the ground, but a pathway nonetheless. Several older beings are filing into this setting. Dustiness in the air, they are filing through that dust and sit on this curved bench. They appear to me translucent, fluid, not dense beings, not solid forms.

John has more whiteness to his presence than the others, who seemed to have a more grayish tone. He is standing in the center of this garden setting. He is the sage. He has the more powerful, authoritarian presence of the group. I get a big hug from John. He sits next to me with his arm over my shoulder, if there is a shoulder. It seems to be a welcoming moment. They are all happy to have me back. I hear the words that let me know that I did well. I feel a lot younger than John. In relative terms, he is ancient to my youth. He is like the spiritual grandfather to me.

We are taking off now, left the welcome garden, and we are flying. John is taking me back to the dark forest, sitting me down on the rock. The rock is bright white while everything else is dark. "This is different" I heard myself say many times throughout this second odyssey. Crying, I say, "Here comes the Light again." There is a pause of undetermined time before I somewhat gain my composure I say that it is very bright; it is so bright that it hurts my eyes. After a long pause, I seem to be experiencing much more than I am reporting to Susan. Jesus is with me, but it is as though we are communicating with each other, without words, inside the bright white light.

Next, I find myself in some kind of soul shower, not water, but glittering light. I hear myself say to Susan that it is almost like a carwash, cleansing me in every way. All is sparkling now. Dr. Newton (1994) speaks of *soul restoration* in a way that resembles this mystical shower moment.

Actually, more occurred here than the recording picked up. In other words, more happened than I reported to Susan, but definitely remained in my superconscious memory bank. At the end of the session, when we were reflecting on the experiences, I heard myself say that the shower was part of a many step cleansing process. It was like the scene in the Wizard of Oz, where the main characters received spa-like makeovers, ending up cleaned and fluffed and sparkling.

John is coming back into the scene, and we are flying towards a distant, very powerfully bright light. I am now hovering very close to the light, and I feel as though a form of light is being created. It seems like John is watching what is happening to me from a distance. Out of no form in me brcomes a being of light coming directly from the Creator's light substance. I can see the edge of this shimmering light form – me!

Light And The Soul

I must interject that I recently read a book on conscious awareness by a natural-born scientist named Dr. Robert Lanza. Having studied under Skinner, Salk and

Barnard, Dr. Lanza has been exploring the frontiers of science for over forty years and is presently the Chief Scientific Officer at Advanced Cell Technology and is an Adjunct Professor at Wake Forest University School of Medicine. In his book, *Biocentrism* (2009), he describes all sorts of notions of what and how we are aware of our existence and surroundings.

One of the concepts that Dr. Lanza (2009) shared near the end of his book is eerily close to what I have just described. He was talking about what one would be aware of if one were moving at the speed of light. He said that one would feel as though one was stationary (similar to my hovering) and that directly in front of us would be All That Is coming together as a bright ball of light (similar to how I described the Creator's light).

The irony here is that Dr. Lanza is describing something that he deems purely scientific, and does not bother to mention the word God in his description. But those of us who think of God, think of God as being omnipresent, All That Is. So, all that is coming together as this brilliant ball of light is really both scientific and spiritual at the same time. It need not be considered just one or the other.

Returning To The Second Odyssey.

Continuing, I am now in what looks like a tanning bed with bright light bombarding me from all directions, creating all the energy of me, all light, as bright as the Creator's light. I have to say that this was in a linear context very hard to witness, but in the celestial realm, it was as natural a phenomenon as one could experience. Rudolph Steiner adds a bit of context here, which I did not come across until years after this odyssey. Steiner believed, from his decades of spiritual research, that the soul spends time in three particular domains between lives. He said that we first go to a lunar place that is not too different from the earthly experience. Then we spend time in a solar place, where we are better able to understand our Christ-like natures. And lastly, before returning to a new life in the earthly realm, we spend time in the cosmos, where we are bombarded with light energy (Steiner, 1968).

Until reading Steiner's work, I could not really answer the question of why would I need more light bombardments after being born directly out of the Creator's light energy? I am still not sure where I stand on this point, but at least there is a sensible thought from Steiner to consider.

My next scene is that of a shooting star, comet-like sensation and vision. I hear myself say that I am a light trail. I am racing through outer space. With the eyes closed I see darkness. With open eyes, everything that I am passing through is bright. I am in an outer space of brightness, not darkness. Again, if I close my eyes, there is darkness, and I am the light that is going through it.

Now I have come into a hospital room. It is an all-white delivery room, and I see my mother. This is wild and now emotional as I see myself in her embryonic sack, the sack is now filled with a being of light. I seem to be in a hurry to come out, not because of any physical discomfort, but I am in a hurry to come completely out. I am ready to get going in this new life.

I hear Susan ask me what am I here to learn in this lifetime, and I immediately respond that I am coming to teach and heal. I am not here to learn but to teach. It seemed a bit harsh as I heard this response to Susan. Then I was asked, "Why did you choose this mother?" My response was, "Because she was ready for me, she wanted me." I guess that I picked a willing mother.

Upon reflection, the losing of my brother was just my door to the monastery. The first time through, I now see that I missed being the Abbot of the monastery with the teaching and leading and healing. I thought that I was alone, but never was alone. There is a lot more to the original story than I realized on my first time through it. The monks loved and respected me more than I realized. My life was not about sadness and penance, I was not the cause of my brother's departure.

The most significant understandings from this second odyssey had to do with two things:

1) Seeing the illuminated, metallurgical event of the creating of the spiritual energy being as me, which lives in the human form that was created for me by my human parents, and

2) My real purpose in that lifetime was being in the monastery as teacher and leader of the monastic community.

That is an expanded impression from my first perception of that life. My real purpose in this present lifetime was presented to me, perhaps even by me, as I heard myself say to go out and teach. Teach love and heal. Repeat what you or I did in the monastery, but this time, do it out in the world.

As the session was coming to an end, I realized that this second odyssey did not contradict anything from the first viewing, but filled in details that I could not have guessed would come up. All through the session I kept praying to the Voice to show me what You want me to see, but do not let me make anything up.

I saw the same light, but was aware of how my entry into it was much faster and more natural than the first viewing. The dark forest had a very white rock for sitting. Then I knew that I was that same light and saw mostly the light of Jesus Christ, more than the human-like form.

This experience was more about showing us the reshaping of the Divine me, and how that birth truly preceded the human birth that I was so humbly and gratefully allowed to witness. There are truly two miracles of birth, not just one. Finally and with utmost humility I say that the Voice wanted me to know that I was made as They wanted me to be with all that I needed for this coming lifetime. The extra light that I was shown seems to be the Voice saying that I have more than enough light to do what I am intended to do in the coming incarnation in the earthly realm. My Divine purpose in this lifetime is clearly to teach love and by doing so, heal brothers and sisters of the light, and that is precisely what I am doing.

The Voice has gone out of Its way to show us these graciously mystical understandings. It seems that contrary to common knowledge, we are supposed to know that we are soulfully immortal and that we come into human existence with clearly defined purposes. It is up to us to discover our purpose and live Divinely in accordance with it. And furthermore, we need to know that the Voice is always here to assist us on our way.

From the past life of the Abbot, I might add that I was there to assist those who were passing into the next realm. I felt such a connection to these people and their families. Perhaps what I did with Lou and Florence will become a bigger part of this life.

The brightness of the light as considered in association with sparkly gold vestments really seemed to bother my understanding of this monastic setting. Looking at myself saying mass at the altar, I was perplexed by the glistening golden light.

We will understand this once in our next viewing of this between life. Asked by Susan how this feels, I replied that there was a powerful sensation that felt enormously out of context.

THIRD ODYSSEY.

Here begins the third odyssey of between lives. From the light of the Abbot's deathbed and into the celestial, I landed on a mountain top with a spectacular panoramic view, all encompassing, nothing blocking the splendor, smoky, dusty colors of wave-like functions, dusty shades of burgundy, blue, green, purple, and red, with a softness to the colors. There was no thing there; and yet, there was this wave-like vision of these dusty colors. It was like everywhere and no-where at the same time.

Then I noticed the presence of someone sitting with me, who seemed to be enjoying this endless view with me. Quite emotionally, I say to Susan that it feels like a twin, just like me, sitting with me. We had this very strong feeling of accomplishment. It is hard to describe how very good it feels sitting with this being. Whatever we just did, we felt really good about it. That is what I am sensing and feeling. We are like partners. We did it!!

Next, I am flying again, approaching a powerful golden brightness. There is a presence with me as I approach this brightness. Before I went into this golden light, I felt like I was being welcomed into it, but once I got there, I sensed as though it was me who was inviting me into this light. A non-visible presence welcomed me into the light, and now I am getting acquainted with it. This is golden light, and the energy that welcomed me is *me*.

The golden energy then took me back to the monastic church setting and everything is of the golden light. What was golden on the altar that I could not understand in the past life is now everything, and is this same golden color. The same is true for the hospital beds that I visited. My death scene room was golden as well, not brilliant white light, but golden light. Instead of feeling weepy from the unconditional love of the pure white light, the golden light produces the feeling of power, of creation. It is an incredibly awesome feeling! There is unlimited strength in it. You have the power. It is you. Feel as strong as you are. Feel your own strength. It is the power given to us by the Divine. We do not believe that we have it, but I am here to say that it is *Us*.

There is no *when*. Stop questioning. I am not differentiated from this golden light. In the second odyssey, I watched myself being created by the light. This time, I am this creative light; and yet, I *know* that I am not the Creator. I am the same as this golden energy, but recognize my reverence for *That which created me*. There is a subtle but beautiful difference between creating and being the creation.

I find myself asking for direction, "What do You want me to do with this power?" Very, very strong messages are coming back to me as I am crying from the very center of my being. God, the Creator is saying, "Everything that you are doing is of the Creator, so do not concern yourself with what you are supposed to do with this power. Just keep doing what intuition says to do."

God is doing the *doing*. God is saying this in such a beautiful way. When we surrender to God, we are doing His or Her work. What God intends us to do is what He or She is doing through us. This is a very big relief from the pressure coming from the questions of what am I supposed to be doing, and am I living right. Enormous weights are being lifted off of our shoulders!! But that is the Divine beauty of surrender. We do not really surrender at all because we are already Divine. But, we do need to make the reverent statement that we let go of our personal will to allow us to be in the flow of Divine will. We do have the choice of which flow to be. One is noticeably Divine, while the other is noticeably human. Which do we choose? God is patient. We all eventually choose to allow the Divine will to be our flow. It is just a matter of when.

Sometimes we say that we are the vessel, meaning that our body is the vessel. But what we learned today is that we are the Divine vessel, not the body as vessel, but the soul as vessel for God. I am reminded of words that I frequently shared with Florence, "I am never what I think I am, but always what I truly am, the indwelling host of God, the Creator." Once we have surrendered to God's will, then we no longer even have to ask or wonder what we are supposed to be doing. We just go with the Divine flow. It should be effortless on our parts. This is not laziness. It is totally trusting God's plan. It is not like we can script this anyway. This lesson is about Divine Surrender. We just stay fine and stay in the Divine flow.

I heard myself say to Susan that I do not think that I can take much more of this light for now, that we should probably bring me out of this energy. I am not usually worn out from these odysseys, and this was after only about eighty or ninety minutes. The Voice spoke so powerfully to me this time. My physicality took all that it could take for the time being.

REFLECTIONS AND CLARIFICATIONS WITH SUSAN

Each time through the odyssey was beautiful, but this third time was much stronger than the others. The loop back through the golden light of the monastery was like a re-orientating tour. All that was perplexing to me in the past life became unquestionably clear to me. The golden light was who I Am, who we all are meant to know that we are. The powerful Voice then was asking me, "Why do you keep asking? Why do not you accept the Truth of your Divinity? Yes, you did not create your Divinity, but you are Divine!!"

I was crying from my core. The message was so very powerful!! Susan's intuition told her that my grappling in the past life would be answered in the between life, and it surely was. So, as not to sound or feel delusional, I knew that I had not created the golden light, but at the same time, I knew that I was the golden light.

I never truly knew what surrender meant the way I did when in the golden light. The recognition of the Divine connection was key. When you say the word surrender, and really mean the word, then you recognize that you already are what you hope to be, One with God. This experience truly supports what

I have been telling people about surrender. But now, having experienced the golden light, and experiencing the truest meaning of surrender, I can speak with true authority on this subject.

Susan just now said, "That golden light is still all around you."

In a strange way, I saw myself skate past the garden scene this time through. I did the same with the bright Christ light on my second time through. These were real experiences in the first and second odysseys. They were not absent from the third one, but they did not need to be re-examined again. The Voice knew that we had seen and understood these prior moments. In a way, it was comforting to see that they were there again, but truly unnecessary for us to re-visit, when so much news was there to be witnessed. And, we surely did.

At the same time, I am sensing that if you are willing to keep visiting the soul life, you will be given more to see. That is, if you are dedicated to knowing the Truth, the Voice will show you more and more. This is another one of those choices that we make. A teacher once said that nature likes to hide from us. Having been on these three odysseys, I can proclaim with authority that absolutely nothing is truly hidden from us. It is all here, in its grandest splendor, to be seen and heard, to be enjoyed and appreciated. However, we must take the step of wanting to see what is here for us. By setting authentic intentions to be with God in the deepest way, we are invited into the most mystical of realms.

Concluding Thoughts And Moments

As we are about to wrap up our discussion of the odysseys of between lives, I must share with you something remarkable that is taking place. There has been a weeklong interruption to this writing. No, we were not on vacation, or sick, or needing a break. But, the Voice did send me to a very sacred place, where a dear friend was about to make her transition to the place between lives. You might say that the Voice was putting a stamp on our understanding of this powerful experience that we are discussing.

The few days before I received the call that a dear friend had entered the hospital with incurable illness, I noticed that my body was vibrating at an unusually high level. It became obvious to me, when I sat down with my friend, that I was transmitting this energy to her. She felt it, and it definitely brought her comfort. We spoke not of where she had been in her life, but of where she was headed in the celestial realm.

In much the same way that I shared these mysteries with Florence over nearly five years of Thursdays, I shared these same mysteries with Vida in a three-day crash course, called for and sponsored by the Voice. She listened intently and responded that she felt a great resonance with these words and concepts. From where she lay, she knew the Truth that the Voice was sharing with her.

Still, she was not quite ready to go. She desperately wanted a bit more time with her children. I arrived at the hospital one morning with Vida saying that she felt very strange. She could not put into words what she was experiencing, but I knew that it was real to her. Not much time passed before the angels came for her, and I say this literally, not figuratively. She sat up in her bed, saw what only her eyes could see, waved them away and said, "No, I want more time with my children." The angels granted her wish and back into her body she went, writhing in pain, but patiently awaiting the arrival of her children.

One child arrived from a distant part of the country, and the other two joined her in her hospital room, where the physical pain that was turning into a loving light was clearly evident. The energy of the children's laughter and reflections and unconditional love for each other was impossible to miss. All was Divinely well in this little family as Vida made her passing, not a passing from life to death, but a passing from life to life, from her life in the earthly realm to her life in the celestial realm.

At the memorial service I mentioned that throughout the week with Vida, I had worn an ancient Greek coin around my neck. It is called the Taras coin and displays a dolphin carrying a person across the sea from shore to shore, which is exactly the energy that I felt was there between Vida and me. The other side was the same person sitting upon a horse, a horse that Vida road peacefully into the sunset. Thank you, Vida, for inviting us into your inner circle just in time to share the amazing beauties and mysteries of your passing. Or should we say, thank you Voice.

I have to say that the Voice spoke quite convincingly to us in these odysseys of between lives. It is one thing to hear the Voice in the earthly realm and quite another thing to hear in the celestial realm. The messages are much clearer and more direct. The visions are much more memorable and spectacular. The Source of the communications is more readily apparent and somehow more natural to hear and behold than on the earthly plane. The brilliant white and golden lights are almost physically unbearable; and yet, we are excitedly drawn to them.

The stages that souls go through in the celestial realm are as easily distinguishable as stages that humans go through on earth. Spiritual scientists have studied these stages in much the same way as physical scientists have studied the evolution of our universe. While the near-death experience was about remembering life's purpose and choosing to return to it, the between-life experience is about being told exactly what our particular life purpose actually is. We are shown that we are actively involved in the setting of the purpose and intentions for the coming life.

It is also about seeing and understanding our relationship with God. We get to know that we are supported and assisted here and in the beyond by guides and angels and one another. We are shown just how Divine we truly are, and how we could actually be One with God and with each other. Also, while we understood the miracle of the life that seems so temporary, we are "blown away" by the permanence of our preceding spiritual birth.

If we are of the Creator's light, and It is everlasting, then how could we be anything less? These are magnificent mysteries coming into a Knowingness that is so beautiful to remember, and remember we do each time we cross beyond our intellects and into the space where all is truly Known.

THE BUDDHA AND BETWEEN LIVES

The Buddha does not speak directly about between lives, as he did not know about past lives. However, he does share words with us that come remarkably close to what we have just heard on this subject from the Voice.

From the verse called, "The Elephant," Buddha states,"It is good to have friends when friendship is mutual. Good deeds are friends at the time of death. But best of all is going beyond sorrow" (Easwaran, 1985, p. 225). These words strike me hard when I think about the last moments with Florence, Lou and Vida.

From the verse called, "Punishment," Buddha says, "As irrigators guide water to their fields, as archers aim arrows, as carpenters carve wood, the wise shape their lives" (Easwaran, 1985, p. 145). The shaping of our lives comes with the assistance of the Voice and those chosen to help us. The viewing of the time between lives is incredibly helpful to our playing out what we already had intended for our lives to be.

From the verse called, "Age," the Buddha notes,

I have gone through many rounds of birth and death, looking in vain for the builder of this body. Heavy indeed is birth and death again and again! But now I have seen you, house builder; you shall not build this house again. Its beams are broken; its dome is shattered: self-will is extinguished; nirvana is attained. (Easwaran, 1985, p. 151)

Having been in the golden light with the Creator, I have some trouble connecting with the tone that the Buddha uses when referring to the house builder. My gratitude for the body that I have been given and the opportunities to come back in service of the Children of the Creator, has undoubtedly come through my time in the white and golden lights. Still, self-will was extinguished in favor of my surrender to the Will of God. So, the Buddha and I must share some of this glorious feeling.

From the verse called "Self," it is stated,

Learn what is right; then teach others, as the wise do. Before trying to guide others, be your own guide first. It is hard to learn to guide oneself. Your own self is your master; who else could be? With yourself well controlled, you gain a master very hard to find. (Easwaran, 1985, p. 157)

I seem to have been shown a short-cut to the guiding of myself. The between-life odyssey, compliments of the Voice, stated quite clearly what I am to teach and share with others in this lifetime. The moment of my ultimate surrender to the Creator then brought me into the lights of unconditional love and power where Divine Order is all that matters.

From the verse called, "Self," Buddha admonishes, "Do not neglect your own duty for another, however great. Know your own duty and perform it" (Easwaran, 1985, p. 158). This is an important point that the Buddha is making here. We come into this lifetime with a specific purpose in mind. It is incredibly important that we not allow ourselves to be sidetracked by other people's projects when ours is to be completed. First things first. Your purpose is your duty. Honor it and help others along the way. But, do take care of your business in this lifetime, or you will have to come back and try again.

From the verse called, "Anger, the Buddha reflects, "But who can blame those who are pure, wise, good, and meditative? They shine like a coin of pure gold. Even the gods praise them, even Brahma the Creator (Easwaran, 1985, p. 189). This helps us understand the powerful nature of the golden light that I referred to in my story. Of course Brahma, the

Creator enjoys seeing the golden light of the Children who have found their way to it. What parent would not be proud of such an achievement?

From the verse called, "The Brahmin," Buddha teaches, "The one I call Brahmin who has gone beyond good and evil and is free from sorrow, passion and impurity. The one I call Brahmin who has crossed the river difficult and dangerous to cross, and safely reached the other shore" (Easwaran, 1985, p. 251). The Taras coin that I wore with Vida was indicative of our crossing the difficult river and safely reaching the other shore. Vida understood where she was headed. Clearly, she asked the angels for just one more day with her children. The Voice thinks of us as the Buddha thought of the Brahmins. We are that special, and so we are guided and supported Divinely.

CHAPTER 9
Santa Monica Moment

▲ ▲ ▲

I WAS IN SANTA MONICA, California, for the fourth meeting of a group of students. All were pursuing advanced degrees in spiritual psychology. I have to say that I never truly understood exactly why I was there. Having already earned my Master of Arts degree in Education and happily teaching math at the college level, I was not looking for another master's degree, and I was not looking for a career change out of teaching. However, I certainly felt called to be there the first weekend of each month. The deeply spiritual interactions with fellow students brought incredibly warm feelings to me. I sensed that many of these students would contribute greatly to the reduction of suffering in the world. But first, many needed to tend to their own broken wings. Somehow, I felt on each flight home, that I had been helping them mend their wings so that they could fly again.

On this particular weekend, I arrived with some extra time on Friday afternoon. Usually, I arrived just in time to check into my hotel and hurry off to class. As I would soon learn, the extra time would be used up in a most incredible manner. I checked into my hotel and headed down to its restaurant. As I sat there, gazing out the window at those passing by, I was overcome with incredibly horrifying feelings of anguish, terror, purposelessness, despair, lostness, and much, much more. Needless to say, these were more than uncomfortable feelings. They were unrecognizable feelings, in that, I was coming from a spiritual place where these feelings did not truly exist. So, in effect, I was witnessing inside of me feelings that were very much foreign to me, but they were there nonetheless.

I could not eat. I arose and went for a walk to try to release these feelings. As I walked, I reminded myself that I was the lighthouse, so how could I feel lost? The walk was not successful in shaking loose these feelings.

I grabbed my swimsuit and went to the local YMCA to see if I could clear my head. The water has always been my special place of calming and resuscitation. But again, the thoughts would not let go of me.

I went back to my hotel room and called my wife. She heard the horror in my voice and tried her best to help me shake free. Suddenly, out of nowhere, the Voice entered this picture. I sensed that the ego was mourning its demise. I had recently received a crash course in death, with a dozen or so people, each in a different way related to me, having passed away. I had been with them before, during or after their passing. So, the feeling of mourning was not unfamiliar to me. I had no idea when ego thought it would pass, but suddenly I felt released of my deep suffering. As quickly as it had come on, it was now gone. Wow, what a relief!!

That night and the whole next day were a bit of a blur. I went through the motions and made my way to Sunday's class. Our morning exercise was going to be terrific. We were going to a very deep place within to witness a conversation between our ego and our Higher Self. I thought, "This should be interesting!" With no trouble, I was in my deepest place and waited for the conversation to begin. I waited and waited and finally, only one Voice came up, and it most certainly was not the voice of the ego. First came the words, "Jesus, John, Joshua are One." Next came the visual of the Creator's ball of brilliant light creating my light form (from the second odyssey of between lives). Next came the words, "I am a Son of God." Next came the words, "I bring Peace to mankind." And finally came the words, "I never really left." (*Notice that the pronoun throughout is I and not You. It comes across as a most unusual form of Voice. Usually, we are being spoken to. This time, the "I" was doing the talking*).

Upon hearing the final words, I was whisked into an ecstatic state, one that lasted quite some time. I was flying through the air and swimming through the sea with unlimited abandon. I felt such a powerful sense of the ultimate freedom of which we only dream. Although I continued to go through the motions for the next several days, I do not believe that I truly left that state. Fortunately for me, it was time for a long lunch break.

I walked around Santa Monica in this amazing state. Everyone that I came across was beautiful. Everyone was love. Couples together, children with parents and grandparents, dogs and cats, all were in the light. I offered a twenty-dollar bill to an elderly woman who was sitting on the sidewalk. At first she was not aware of the size of the bill. When she noticed, she looked up at me with such gratitude. Her eyes were sparkling in such a glorious way. I felt so intimately connected to everyone that I came across.

I returned to the classroom in time to resume the course work. But, I was truly just going through the motions. I was in such a non-linear state of being. Without mentioning any of what I had experienced, students seemed to know that something very different was occurring. Looking directly into the eyes of women and even male classmates brought them to tears. During a three-person conversation, one of them said to the other, "We are talking with the Buddha, really, we are talking with the Buddha!!"

I could not wait to get home to share all that I had experienced with my wife. This life would truly never be the same. And of course, it was never meant to be. As we learned from the between-life odysseys, I was to teach love and heal. So, this life had just truly begun anew!

Ministries Multiplied

My first spiritual book flew out of me, sharing Divine fingerprints of choices and callings and unconditional love. Speaking weekly at Unity Church came forth. Spending time with the elderly became a weekly event. A spiritual study group grew in very deep ways. The Voice came louder and more frequently. It was almost impossible to keep track of the visions and understandings. We just started sharing what was coming forth in whatever way seemed most sensible. People began showing up for past and between life sessions and many other forms of counseling. Hospital visits came all too often.

All of the preceding chapters of experiences came to life in vivid color, and were really just the tip of the spiritual iceberg. The Voice was sending us on a whirlwind tour of people, places and things. All was connected in the most Divine ways. We were surrounded by spiritual breakthroughs of all sorts and from all directions. The linear and non-linear worlds mixed with great frequency. The spiritual dimensions and paradigms overlapped continuously. All that was experienced was to be shared, at least it always seemed to me, and we happily continue to do so.

REFLECTIONS FROM THE BUDDHA

The Buddha has much to say about the enlightened state. I just see the world as it truly is without the fearful limitations that the ego puts on it. The Voice reminds me to just stay in the Divine flow and let Divine order proceed.

From the verse called, "The Wise," the Buddha states, "Well trained in the seven fields of enlightenment, their senses disciplined and free from attachments, they live in freedom, full of light" (Easwaran, 1985 p. 127). Freedom is the ultimate reward for whatever it takes to discover this glorious state. The white and golden lights are always with me.

From the verse called, "The Path," Buddha acknowledges the best,

Of paths the Eightfold is the best; of truths the Noble Four are the best; of mental states, detachment is the best; of human beings, the illumined one is best. Now is the time to wake up, when you are young and strong. Those who wait and aver, with a weak will and a divided mind, will never find the way to pure wisdom. (Easwaran, 1985, pp. 205-206)

The illumined one is best because with it comes freedom, and so, why wait? Why not search for the Truth that sets you free?

From the verse called, "Varied Verses," Buddha notes, "If one who enjoys a lesser happiness beholds a greater one, let him leave aside the lesser to gain the greater" (Easwaran, 1985, p. 211). This is the most natural of reactions when one is shown the realm beyond. It is why the near-death experiencer balks at returning until love calls him or her back to the earthly realm.

Again, from the verse called, "Varied Verses," Buddha advises,

Sitting alone, sleeping alone, going about alone, vanquish the ego by yourself alone. Abiding joy will be yours when all selfish desires end. Those who are good and pure in conduct are honored wherever they go. The good shine like the Himalayas, whose peaks glisten above the rest of the world even when seen from a distance. Others pass unseen, like an arrow shot at night. (Easwaran, 2985, p. 213)

In my experience, it is really not about the good versus the bad, nor the pure versus the impure. It is more about the surrendered versus those holding onto their personal wills. It is like parental advice that children do not seem to follow. When I say that to surrender brings unimaginable freedom, peace and joy, what is there left for you to say?

From the verse called, "Thirst," Buddha states,

If you want to reach the other shore of existence, give up what is before, behind, and in between. Set your mind free and go beyond birth and death. If you want to reach the other shore, do not let doubts, passions and cravings strengthen your fetters. Meditate deeply, discriminate between the pleasant and the permanent, and break the fetters of Mara. I have conquered myself and live in purity. I know all. I have left everything behind, and live in freedom. Having taught myself, whom shall I point as teacher? (Easwaran, 1985, p. 236)

Well, well, there is an awful lot that the ego puts in your way of finding the boat, much less safely crossing to the other shore. The good news is that all that is in your way is illusion, Mara. None of what stops you from crossing is real. But all that stops you seems real and frightening. However, believe me when I say, "Surrender to your Creator and discover that you have all the guidance and support to find your way to freedom, which has been there all along."

From the verse called, "The Brahmin," the Buddha speaks of self will,

That one I call Brahmin who has risen above duality of this world, free from sorrow and free from sin. Such a one shines like a full moon with no clouds in the sky. Self-will has left his mind; it will never return. Sorrow has left his life; it will never return. (Easwaran, 1985, pp. 251-252)

Duality is the ultimate illusion. The sense of separateness is that upon which the ego thrives. Unity and Oneness is what the ego fears the most, and the closer that you come to It, the more the ego senses its demise, and the harder it fights. The Friday night in Santa Monica was the ego's last chance to dissuade me from my ultimate freedom. But, the Voice was right there with me. Sure, It let me feel the ego's pain one last time, and I must say that it was excruciating! However, this was my last big test, and its outcome was crucial to what the rest of this life would look like for me. If I was really going to teach Love and Surrender, then I was going to have to pass this last test. Passing this test brought the nirvana that the Buddha spoke so highly about. But, that was just a reference point for me. It is something that I can describe but not dissolve into, for I came here with the purpose of teaching Love and Surrender. There will be plenty of time for nirvana when the time comes.

CHAPTER 10
Conclusion

▲ ▲ ▲

WE HAVE NOW LISTENED TO the Voice speak to us through more than sixty thousand words. In my experience, the Voice speaks clearly and directly. It does not sugar coat, mince words, pad thoughts, or beat around the bush. Hence, these sixty thousand words from the Voice have come at us pretty hard. Let us take a moment and quickly review what we heard from the Voice.

SOJOURNS INTO DREAMLAND

The group-dream sharing is the context through which the meaningful messages come to us from the Voice. The entry into sacred space and the unconditional loving efforts that we make to assist the dreamer in understanding meaning in their dreams was brought to us through the Voice. The many layers of meaning that fill each dream became clearer to us through the Voice. That we work in true connection with our fellow man in this endeavor was beautifully shown to us by the Voice. That we are actually healing and helping others in their healing processes, through group dream sharing, is perhaps the greatest news coming from the Voice.

TRIPS INTO ALTERED STATES OF CONSCIOUSNESS

The Voice has clearly led us to understand what shamans and other indigenous peoples have known for a very long time, that healing can occur from within, with the help of a gifted facilitator. Drs. Grof, Bolte Taylor and Alexander have shown us what prior scientists were uncomfortable revealing to us, but surely what the Voice wanted us to see. That there is so much more about living than the scientific community can describe to us, is a powerful message coming to us through the Voice. The orbs of light, shown to us by the Voice in so many ways, seem to carry the energy of the Creator, the energy that is who or what we truly are.

Questing For A Vision

I notice the Voice in every aspect of this powerful story of my vision quest. I notice the Voice in the wisdom that was shared by and though Crazy Horse, Lame Deer, Black Elk and Will Taegel. I notice the Voice in every moment of my vision quest preparation, from the inspiration that I felt to put my stake in the ground, through every prayer bundle that I tied, through every step up and down my hill and other aspects in the ways of my purification of body, mind and spirit. I noticed the Voice through every song that I sang or danced, through every bite of food that I did not eat during the days leading up to and including the quest, through every powerful moment of the quest with the squirrel and the cloud figures and the animated, playful animals, and most importantly, through the mountain lion interaction. I noticed the Voice through the overlapping and confirming vision of my supporter friend, and finally, through the sacred name given to me at the end by my holy person. Every single step along the way seemed to be guided and encouraged by the Voice, leading me through inspiration, dedication, purification, collaboration, and finally, through appreciation for all that was presented to or through me. All that is meant to be presented to or through me in the many years to come, as my new name suggests.

Adventures In The Afterlife

There is no doubt in my mind that the Voice was not only present, but active in the orchestration of my participation in Lou's and Florence's passing, in the hospital with Bernadette's son-in-law, and with all those visited by departed loved ones. The Voice is responsible in what is experienced and learned in near-death and shared-death experiences, for sure. It is not just that we are shown something mysterious, but that the lives of the experiencers are so dramatically changed for the better. This is certainly not a new phenomenon, as the Voice has clearly been facilitating such conversations since at least the time of the ancient Greeks.

Why would that have been the beginning of these incredible conversations? Clearly, the Voice has been assisting us since times far further back than ancient Greece! This journey that we have been on, through the energies of mirror gazing and other related experiences, was meant to open up our minds to the incredible possibilities that are available to us in this lifetime. Like the experiences of (NDE) and (SDE), we have been shown that life exists far beyond our limited imaginations. When we listen to the Voice of Divinity, we are guided to places and feelings that so often become overlooked or lost in the meaningless details of life. These opportunities are not just offered to avatars, prophets and saints. They are offered to each and every one of us. It is up to us to desire the connection with God that opens us up to Truth and Ultimate Freedom.

PILGRIMAGES TO SACRED PLACES

Done properly, these excursions are not for the faint of heart. The very nature of a pilgrimage requires courage, dedication and devotion. It is my perception that the Voice is at the very heart of all of these spiritual qualities. It is the Voice that inspires our desire to be a pilgrim. The Voice fills our wills with what we need to handle the stresses of these powerful journeys. The Voice fills our eyes and ears with messages throughout these sacred journeys, whether in Chartres, Sedona, Teotihuacan, or anywhere else in this world. Furthermore, the Voice inspires us to share the glory of what we saw and heard during these powerfully mystical moments of pilgrimage.

VOYAGES INTO PAST LIVES

The Voice has been with these voyages and every single moment of past-life visitation, as far as I am concerned. How I was introduced to this subject and have been encouraged by these experiences are attributed to the Voice. The knowingness that surrounded each encounter, as guide or as guided, is through the Voice. The nature of the innocence of thought as revealed by the linear versus non-linear thinking can only come from the Voice. The layers of revelation that came through the three succeeding voyages to the very same life were mystical gifts from the Voice. That we can find wisdom and healing in this lifetime through visits to past lives can only come through the grace of the Voice.

Some ask me, do you think that we are supposed to see and know these things? My answer, without question, is that the Voice is what is speaking to us through these visits. If we were not intended to see these past lives, then why would we be shown them? Bigger than that though, is the sense that the Voice wants us to expand this healing modality. It seems to be a gift that is truly meant to keep on giving. And so, we shall.

ODYSSEYS BETWEEN LIFE, AFTER-LIFE, AND THE CELESTIAL REALM

The Voice is working, not with our bodies and minds in this realm, but with our souls. The sensations are much more vivid and spectacular. The mind that is active during these sessions is the superconscious mind, operating in the deep vibration of the theta waves. We are experiencing the re-living of these soulful moments and able to comment on them at the same time. We are truly in two dimensions, simultaneously. The Voice has our full attention. As with multiple voyages to the same past life, multiple odysseys to the same between life bring clarity and expanded understandings from differing points of emphasis from the Voice. Welcoming from my long-time guide (John) along with soul mates and council members, mystical gardens, crystal mountains, showers of loving light, reflections on the recent life's experiences, visits to magnificent dimensions, plans and preparations for the future life, infusing with Light, and special messages from the Voice were all personal experiences of my soul and elements of what Dr. Newton and Dr. Steiner heard from decades of soulful research.

The Voice knows what to focus our attention on each time through our lives. Watching carefully, I knew that moments from the first and second odysseys were available to me in the third. But, there was really no need to re-visit or re-examine. The clearest message that was supposed to come through from the Voice clearly is what came through each time. Worthiness and purpose came through the first odyssey. The double miracles of birth came through the second. The Oneness with God, brought forward through Divine Surrender, came through the third odyssey.

Finally, the application of all this wisdom and understanding was able to flow seamlessly, when called to spend time with Vida. The Voice was truly saying that it is one thing to know and quite another to share these mysteries of the soul.

Conclusion

Having reviewed these magnificent journeys to the sacred place and heard directly what the Voice had for us, let us take an important step back and view the breadth of this landscape even more deeply. As we said earlier, any one of these journeys by itself was deep and would have inspired us to make changes in how we perceive the world and how we hope to live our lives in this world. However, the full array of modalities that the Voice uses as It speaks to and through us is almost more than we can handle. But, of course, we can.

We are not given more than we can handle, but it is up to us to make the first choice. We must choose to surrender our personal will to the power of the Divine will. We must see that we are not only part of humanity, but One with humanity and One with Divinity. Knowing more about our Divine nature, we must now live in accordance with it. We must let go of the fearful thoughts and perceptions and allow the Divine flow to flow through Us, *Divinely*. We can use any or all of these Divinely spiritual modalities to help ourselves and others, as we heal body and soul.

As we have seen, many times we use overlapping spiritual modalities at the same time. Dreams or meditations can easily flow into a psst-life scene and back into the dream or meditative place. We saw that the orbs came through a number of spiritual modalities. Pilgrimages bring us into powerful vortexes of wisdom where any of these spiritual modalities can arise. The Voice spoke in a powerful between-life scene and then again through the Santa Monica moment. The Voice knows exactly when to underline or stamp a thought that it has already given to us. And of course, the Voice knows when we have received the intended message and when a multiple viewing, particularly across modalities, might be helpful to our knowing. We can and should allow ourselves to follow the lead of the Voice in this regard. We can allow ourselves to weave these modalities together as we see the need in those that we are helping, as the Voice did while helping us.

We are certainly never alone, as this is definitely a group effort. We are given earthly and celestial partners and friends all the way through these lifetimes and between. We are all truly heading in the very same direction and play different roles in each experience. We are the white light of unconditional love and the golden light of powerful creation. We do not just revel in these lights, but share them with all that come our way. We are filled with humility and gratitude for what we are allowed to see and know.

The Voice is beyond generous with us, and we are keenly aware of the gifts of grace that we receive. In the final analysis, we hear the Voice, and we speak the Voice. We are more than just Divine listeners, we speak the Voice, and I truly believe that this is why the Voice has spoken so clearly to us. We are expected to speak the Voice for all to hear. And so, we speak the Voice.

BUDDHA'S PRESENCE

The Buddha entered this Divine discovery as a means of magnifying our mystical experiences. We are grateful for His presence in this writing. We all know that the Buddha had the most selfless of intentions in His quest to end human suffering. The devotion and dedication that He showed in His lifetime has inspired us for more than twenty-five hundred years. It was a pleasure to see and hear the conversation that took place between the Voice and the Buddha. We are privileged to have witnessed the connections between two such powerful energies.

Yet, as we look around, we notice that many of us continue to suffer. Is this because we are not following the Buddha's Way? Is the Buddha's Way too difficult for us? Do we even understand the Buddha's Way? I guess that I would answer, "Yes," to all of the above. The Buddha spoke so often of the Mind and our need to surrender to it through deep meditation. *The Dhammapada* was filled with worthwhile and inspiring advice from the Buddha.

However, what I continue to hear from the Voice of Divinity is that the Mind is not the intellect, and so the intellect is not the answer to our suffering. The intellect is a powerful tool that we can use as we attempt to navigate through and investigate our spectacular universe. But in a most mystical way, the Voice has always pointed me beyond the intellect to the sacred place where all true Wisdom resides.

LISTENING TO THE VOICE

The Voice has pointed me to many powerfully mystical moments, the most prominent being my ultimate surrender to God, the Creator, in the golden light. The white light of unconditional love was spectacular, as anyone who has been there can attest. The golden light is the truest light, the light of power, the light of creativity, the Light of the Creator. It is the place where all are One, where peace, love, joy and harmony exist so naturally. It is the place of our ultimate freedom, where suffering exists only as an illusion.

The choice is yours, and has always been. Perfect your understanding of and practice of the Buddha's Way, and you will most likely find your ultimate freedom. Or, listen to what the Voice is telling us right now. Surrender your will to God. Let go of your attachments to everything except your love for your Creator and discover the freedom that comes with the Divine flow. Accept your Divine inheritance and live your life in accordance with your own true Divinity.

Namaste, Peace, Love, Light, and *Mitakuye Oyasin*, my dear friends.

Divine Power Speaks

Alexander, E. (2012). *Proof of heaven*. New York: Simon & Schuster.

Barasch, M. I. (2000). *Healing dreams*. New York: Riverhead Books.

Black Elk, W. (1991). *Black Elk: The sacred ways of a Lakota*. New York: HarperCollins.

Bolte Taylor, J. (2006). *My stroke of insight: A brain scientist's personal journey*. New York, NY: Viking Penguin Group.

Campbell, J. (1987). *The hero's journey: A biographical portrait*. USA, London, England: A Mythology Ltd. with Pantechnicon Productions.

Critchlow, K. (2003). *Chartres cathedral: A sacred geometry*. USA: Golden Age Productions.

Easwaran, E. (1985). *The Dhammapada*. Tomales, CA: Nilgiri Press.

Grey, A. (2000). *The visionary artist, visualizations for creative exploration*. Boulder, CO: Sounds True.

Grof, S. (1998). *The transpersonal vision, the healing potential of non-ordinary states of consciousness*. Boulder, CO: Sounds True.

Hawkins, D. (1995). *Power vs. force, The hidden determinants of human behavior*. West Sedona, AZ: Veritas Publishing.

Hawkins, D. (2001). *The eye of the I, From which nothing is hidden.* West Sedona, AZ: Veritas Publishing.

Hawkins, D. (2003). *I, reality and subjectivity.* West Sedona, AZ: Veritas Publishing.

Hawkins, D. (2003). *Enlightenment.* West Sedona, AZ: Veritas Publishing.

Hawkins, D. (2007). *Experiential reality: The mystic.* West Sedona, AZ: Veritas Publishing.

Heraclitus. (July 2011). http: www. Goodreads.com.

Jefferson, W. (2008). *Reincarnation beliefs of North American Indians.* Summertown, TN: Native Voices.

Jowett, B. (2008). *Plato's Phaedo.* Rockville, MD: Arc Manor.

Lame Deer, J. & Erdoes, R. (1994). *Lame Deer: Seeker of visions.* New York: Simon & Schuster.

Lanza, R. (2009). *Biocentrism: How life and consciousness are the keys to understanding the true nature of the universe.* Dallas, TX: Ben Bella Books.

Marshall, J. (2005). *The journey of Crazy Horse.* New York: Penguin Group.

Metcalf, B. (2000). *The shaman's heart II.* Prescott, AZ: BMI and Soundquest Music.

Moody, R. (1975). *Life after life.* New York: HarperCollins.

Moody, R. & Perry P. (2010). *Glimpses of eternity: Sharing a loved one's passage from this life to the next.* New York: Guideposts.

Newton, M. (1994). *Journey of souls: Case studies of life between lives.* Woodbury, MN: Llewellyn Publications.

Prophet, E. (1997). *Reincarnation: The missing link in Christianity.* Corwin Springs, MT: Summit University Press.

Scorsese, M. (2011). *George Harrison, Living in the material world.* Santa Monica, CA: Grove Street Productions.

Spalding, B. (1955). *Life and teaching of the masters of the Far East.* Camarillo, CA: DeVorss Publications.

Steiner, R. (1968). *Life Between death & rebirth.* USA: Anthroposophic Press.

Taegel, W. (2010). *The sacred council of your wild heart: Nature's hope in earth's crisis.* Wimberley, Tx: 2nd Tier Publishing.

Taegel, W. (2012). *The mother tongue: Intimacy in the eco-field.* Wimberley, TX: 2nd Tier Publishing.

Taylor, J. (1983). *DreamWork: Techniques for the creative power in dreams.* Mahwah, NJ: Paulist Press.

Weiss, B. (1988). *Many lives: Many masters.* New York: Fireside Books.

Wisehart, S. (2008). *Soul Visioning, clear the past, create your future.* Woodbury, MN: Llewellyn Publications.